PANOS VALAVANIS

THE HILL
OF THE HIDDEN SECRETS

A chronicle of an imaginary excavation

ILLUSTRATED BY ADA GANOSI

ACTIVITIES BY MARIZA DECASTRO, PANOS VALAVANIS

TRANSLATED BY GEORGIA KOFINAS

AKRITAS
FOR YOUNG READERS

OTHER WORKS FOR CHILDREN BY THE AUTHOR

GREEK POTTERY: A culture captured in clay (with I. Foka) Kedros. 1990, 1992⁶ translated into English, German, French, Swedish.
ARCHITECTURE AND CITY PLANNING (with I. Foka), Kedros 1992, 1995⁵.
ATHENS AND ATTICA: Archaeological Outings, 1997 (I. Foka).
ΑΘΛΑ, ΑΘΛΗΤΕΣ ΚΑΙ ΕΠΑΘΛΑ. ΟΛΥΜΠΙΑΚΟΙ ΑΓΩΝΕΣ ΚΑΙ ΑΘΛΗΤΙΣΜΟΣ ΣΤΗΝ ΑΡΧΑΙΑ ΕΛΛΑΔΑ, Ερευνητές, 1996. [FEATS, ATHLETES AND PRIZES. OLYMPIC GAMES AND ATHLETICS IN ANCIENT GREECE, Erevnites, 1996] (not translated)

BIOGRAPHICAL SKETCH

Panos Valavanis was born in Athens in 1954. He studied History and Archaeology at the University of Athens and at the Archaeological Institute of the University of Würzburg in Germany.

In 1980 he began his career at the University of Athens as a research assistant. In 1988 he became a lecturer, and since 1994 he has held the position of assistant professor of Classical Archaeology and since 2000 as associate professor of classical Archaeology.

His doctorate thesis and most of his studies are concerned with ancient Greek pottery, the architecture and topography of Athens, and ancient Greek athletics technology.

CONTENTS

My dear friends,

The hill with the hidden secrets was not created intentionally. It was the result of thousands of years of various people inhabiting the very same spot. It was in this same spot that they built their houses and temples, the same spot where they lived and died. Hostile invasions, earthquakes and other disasters all took place in the same location.

But the inhabitants were strong and persistent, and rebuilt new cities and villages on the hill burying, each time, the previous remains. So this was what made the hill get bigger and bigger, hiding at the same time all the secrets of the previous inhabitants that had occupied the area.

Centuries went by and the memories were erased by time, yet the hill remained –a hidden and solitary witness of the past. It looked like a volcano that had hidden so many things inside it and was looking for a way to reveal its contents.

One day an archaeologist arrived. He began excavating and slowly started finding the remains of past ages, one layer under the other. Working diligently and patiently he collected the remains of those ancient people's lives and managed to reveal all of their secrets. Thus, was created the history of a great and extraordinary land called Greece.

Panos Valavanis

FROM THE CAVE ERA

We find ourselves somewhere in continental Greece at a time in the past, very long ago, say, about 6000 B.C. A tribe of approximately 250 people –men, women and children– who for many years wandered in the mountains, made an important decision to go further down and build their village near the sea.

These people had lived in the mountains for many generations. It was for so long that even the older tribesmen could barely remember some of the stories their grandfathers had told them. They said that the tribe had come from the North; a place from where the cold north wind blew. These people knew nothing about agriculture or stock-breeding yet, so they were totally dependent on nature for their survival. For this reason they would wander from place to place following the migrating herds of wild animals which they hunted, or moving to those areas where trees yielded seasonal fruit. They spent most of their lives out in the open air, and only at night and in winter did they live in natural shelters such as caves, where they lit fires to see in the dark and keep warm. This is where they did most of their work. The men skinned the wild boars from the day's hunt and cut the meat up to roast over the open fire. The women took the animals' hides and sewed them with needles, made of bone, and grass string to make a warm bed for the newborn babies. During the long winter nights everyone used to sit together –men, women and children– and listen to the stories and tales that the elders narrated.

The more capable men, apart from their regular chores, also had another important duty. They skilfully broke hard stones to make tools, mostly blades for axes and knives which they used to cut weeds or carve meat. Others, who seemed to be more artistic preferred to spend their free time drawing animals on the walls of the caves; probably the animals they wanted to kill on their

TO THE NEOLITHIC REVOLUTION

next hunt. But what they liked doing even more was to fill their mouths with paint and, using a straw, blow it on their hand which they had placed on the wall. That way the cave walls were full of handprints of different colours.

Our story takes us to another corner of the cave where a young man was trying to fix a necklace out of pebbles which he planned to give to the young lady of his choice. Near the entrance a group of women were talking about a new medicinal plant with which they had cured the wound of a hunter's leg. But for the old man who was lying beside them, they knew that no plant could make him stand on his feet again. They took care of him lovingly and when he died, they buried him in a pit outside the cave putting a bouquet of fresh wild flowers on his body.

When there were no caves in the areas they moved to, they set up temporary villages with round huts made of branches, reeds and grass. These huts were unbearably cold in the winter months when the snow fell and everything was white. The living conditions had gotten worse from the time they decided not to light fires at night in the middle of the huts. And this was because one time a small spark had caused a hut to catch on fire and a whole family that was sleeping in it was charred.

Moreover, in these temporary mountain settlements, the people were very often in danger because of the wild animals that lived in the forest. Wolves and bears, when they couldn't find anything to hunt and eat, would come down to the

edge of village and wake up the inhabitants in the middle of the night with their howling.

But the biggest problem the people had to face in the mountain settlement was that their lifestyle had undergone some big changes over the past few years and there was just not enough space left on the mountain. Indeed, just a few years ago the people thought it would be less tiring if, instead of chasing wild goats in the mountains, they caught some young ones, tamed them and kept them near their homes. That way, besides using just their meat and hides as before, they could milk them and drink the milk. And with regular shearing, they could also use the animals' wool. They also thought that it would be better, instead of gathering wild pears, apples and quinces which were a bit sour, to dig up some smaller trees, plant them next to the village and take care of them. That way, they could produce more fruit and it would be tastier.

The greatest need for space was realized when the people started to cultivate grains –wheat and barley. Every year, with the first rains of the season that would later be called Autumn, they ploughed the mountainous land with a wooden plough and then sowed the seeds. By June when the wheat had grown tall and had matured they cut it with wooden sickles which didn't cut well and ruined quickly.

There's one story that says the first seeds of grain were brought to the settlement by a young tribesman who had left the village because, they say, he had an adventurous spirit. The older tribesmen couldn't understand that at the time. The young man travelled far away towards the East to Egypt or somewhere in the Middle East –they couldn't remember that well– but because he found things difficult there he became nostalgic and decided to return to his tribe. Not having anything else to offer them, he brought back some seeds of wheat in a bag and showed them how to cultivate it, then grind it into flour to make man's most staple food –bread!

Despite all the problems and the need for cultivating land, the decision to move the settlement was still not easy. But the elders finally decided to leave after some young men, who had just returned from a long hunt laden with deer, ecstatically narrated their adventures. They listened to the story about the hunters who had stood from a mountain peak and in the horizon they had seen a very large blue surface that shone under the sun's rays. It was very similar to the small lakes they came across every now and then in the mountains, where they liked bending over to look at their reflecion on the calm surface of the water.

After gathering their necessities and whatever they could carry on their shoulders or load on their mules or cows, they all left. They made their way downhill through the even slopes and the cool valleys.

Spring was beautiful. The land was green and the air was filled with the sweet smell of wild flowers. But the people seemed a little skeptical and anxious about perhaps not finding life better in the lowlands.

They walked all day and at dusk they stopped to milk the goats and put the milk in gourds to feed the small children. If they didn't find any fresh hunt on the way, the adults ate the meat that had been preserved in the mountains. This was done by hanging the meat from the roofs of the sheds and smoking it over the fire below.

After a long and tiring journey, while they were passing through a valley next to a calm river, they heard shouts of joy and enthusiasm from the scouts that had been sent ahead. Then they all ran forward and for the first time in their lives they were looking at the sea, close up. They were dazzled by the beauty and the colours, but mostly by the sun that had dived into the sea, painting it with a golden orange colour. They had never seen the sun set in the sea. Up until then, for them the sun had always gone down behind the mountains.

A NEW BEGINNING

They liked the area so much that they decided to set up their village there. It wasn't that they were just fascinated when they saw the area, but after a long conversation among the men, they came to the logical conclusion that this place met all their needs. It was on a slope that would protect them from the cold north winds. It had plenty of fertile land to cultivate, and grass for their animals to graze. Next to them flowed a river with plenty of cool, clean water. The mountains were near enough for them to flee to in the event of danger. Finally, it was near the sea where the coast formed two small bays which could protect their boats from whatever winds the weather brought.

The men quickly started building the houses. They were separated into teams and most of them carried stones from the surrounding mountains. These they used to build the bases of the rectangular houses and construct walls at a height of one metre. From there on up the walls were built with mud-bricks. The men molded them into shape and dried them in the sun. For the roofs they brought thick wood from the forest which they had cut with their stone axes. Tree trunks were also used as columns inside the houses for support.

In the most beautiful area of the settlement they built a large house for the oldest man in the village whom they loved and respected because he was wise and had become their leader. Around the houses they built a high wall to separate the village from the rest of the area. It also served as a way to defend themselves against outside dangers. Around the fields and closer to the sea they set up makeshift straw huts for temporary residence and other uses.

Building the village took a long time, about four months. Besides building

AT THE NEOLITHIC SETTLEMENT

their own houses which every head of the family was responsible for, they also had to help construct the village wall and other community projects.

With the building finished, everyone returned to their daily activities. Most of them became occupied with the land and soon all of the plains and hillsides around the village were cleared, ploughed, sowed and soon sprouting with beautiful green grass. Others were devoted to breeding animals and very soon the hills and stables were filled with the joyous bellows of sheep, goats, cows and pigs of every size and colour. The milk that was left over was gathered in large urns. With this milk the women made different soft and hard cheeses. Very often the men slaughtered a small calf and everyone gathered to feast and dance. In May when the sheep were sheared the people gathered the wool, washed it in the river and afterwards spun it into thread with the distil and spindle. When the thread was made they wove beautiful clothes, rugs and blankets.

The activity in the village was endless. No one, except for the older men, remained idle. The men, whenever they had free time, went hunting. They would wait for the animals and birds at the familiar hunting grounds and then hit them with bows and arrows or clubs. Others preferred to fish either by casting nets over their boats or walking on the beaches with fish spears and hand nets. The women had total responsibility for the house and the children. Not only did they have to do their daily chores, but they also wove fabric on the loom, ground the wheat with handmills and made bread which they baked in the small ovens next to their houses. Some of the more capable women worked with clay and made different vessels, from large urns to small drinking cups which they decorated with beautiful lively colours.

The children of course, liked playing outdoors in large groups. But the older boys went with the men to learn

about agriculture, stock-breeding and the tricks of hunting. The girls stayed close to home with their mothers. The smaller children played in the waters of the river and the sea. They also enjoyed making small dolls out of clay or animals out of cucumbers and squash using small thin sticks for the legs.

Everyone loved the sea. Besides providing fish which was especially tasty, it offered the people something else – a way for the bravest men to travel in their boats to a distant island called Melos to bring back 'obsidian', a hard black volcanic ore. By striking the obsidian in a particular way they made sharp blades for their tools and weapons. Thus they had sharper knives, razors, axes and tips for their spears and arrows. By placing many small blades in a row they made sharper scythes for reaping and better blades for their threshing equipment. They were really lucky to have found obsidian because it helped to increase their production and they became wealthier. Consequently their lives improved, they had more children, increasing the population so that new villages were built. With this, their art and civilization developed, too.

Life went on peacefully until one night something terrible happened. A drunkard went into an area which was considered to be sacred and knocked over an old thick piece of wood which the people had brought down from the mountain and had set up in order to worship it. The next day when everyone found out about it, the wise old man gathered everyone in the middle of the village in front of his house. He looked at each one in the eyes, then slowly and seriously spoke to them in his hoarse voice: "My children, what happened

was very bad. I'm afraid the gods may get angry and send us misfortune". The old man's words were prophetic. Not too much later, suddenly one day a strange noise came out of the earth accompanied by shaking and trembling. Those who were outside looked at each other uneasily, then kept looking up at the sky and down at the earth. Those who were in their houses got out just in time, as a moment after, there was a big tremor. An earthquake! The whole village was brought down to ruins. Only an old lady that couldn't walk had stayed in her house and it seems she was buried by a stone wall. After the horrible catastrophe everyone turned their eyes and their hopes to the wise old man of the village. They expected some words of wisdom from him as he had given them in so many other difficult situations before. He gathered all the men around him while the women and children stood a little further away waiting anxiously for the decision. The tribe had two choices: either to rebuild the village on the same site, or to build somewhere else. The wise old man was quite sure about this – the wrath of the gods may not have ended with this misfortune that struck them. Something worse could happen. So they should move, go to a "purer" area which was "free of sin". And that's what they did. Men, women and children all took their belongings on their backs and set out for a new adventure.

Time passed by, century after century, and a lot of dirt had piled up over the ruins of the village forming a small hill. Whatever was buried and perishable slowly decayed and disappeared. The first items that perished were the straw and fabric, and later the leather, branches, baskets and all the objects made of wood. The rainfalls gradually ate away the walls of the houses and the thick beams from the woodwork collapsed and slowly rotted away.

However, the low stone walls of the houses and the walls remained intact under the dirt. There were other objects that also remained untouched with the passing of time such as stone utensils and tools which the people used, as well as a handmill, a small oven, a stone axe and some other small objects. The clay pots had broken into small pieces when the walls and roofs of the houses collapsed, but they remained in their position. Even the ashes and cinders were preserved, as well as all the bones of the little old lady.

CASTLES AND PALACES

About three thousand years had gone by since the great catastrophe and there was nothing that could be seen on the surface that would reveal the past. The area, however, had not lost the least of its beauty and importance. And so, around 1250 B.C. the Myceneans decided to build a large acropolis on the same exact spot.

It took a long time to build the walls because they had to be very big as well as very strong. And this, because with the discovery and usage of metals which the people learned from the Eastern civilizations in the past, new resistable tools were used to create better weapons. Thus the conditions of wars changed and there was a greater need for protection and defence. So the walls had to be built higher as well as sturdier, not only to discourage the enemy, but also to endure any probable siege. The great stones had to be transported from far away but the Myceneans had developed their technology which they had learned from the more advanced technological skills of the Egyptians and Hittites. In order to lift the large stones up high on the wall they made slopes or ramps out of sand bags. Then on top of these they placed wooden joists on which they dragged the stones by placing wooden cylindrical tumblers underneath. The higher the wall became, the more sand bags they added. When they finished building the wall they removed the sand bags and everything was ready.

On the highest part of the acropolis they built the palace for the king and the royal family. He was lord of all –not only the leader of the country and the army, but also a religious leader, a patriarch. With this title he led the ceremonies. We can just imagine him walking in procession lead by priestesses holding ceremonial vases which they'll offer to the goddess. The procession is

IN THE MYCENEAN ERA

slow and pompous, oblivious to the downpour which suddenly burst out. They're all heading towards the back part of the acropolis, where the religious centre is found, in order to offer a sacrifice.

Meanwhile a ship has come into port from Cyprus. The king, who's also in charge of trade and production, had made a deal with his friend, the king of Cyprus, to import bronze. Cyprus had the best bronze in all the Mediterranean which is firstly refined and then moulded into talents, that is, large plaques weighing approximately 15-17 kilos. These plaques are carried by the stronger men on their shoulders. The Mycenean king later gave the bronze to his craftsmen so they could use their hammers and anvils to make copper weapons for the army (swords, helmets, shields, tips of spears and arrows). A lot of other objects were also made out of the metal and were either used by the people or exported to distant places.

Now, a that time, coins had not been thought up yet and various goods were used for exchange. In exchange for the bronze, the Cypriots were offered scented oils, somewhat like today's perfumes. The Myceneans made these scented oils themselves by mixing olive oil with expensive perfumes they brought from the East. They would then put the mixture in stirrup jars (amphorae with special openings) whose mouth was shaped in such a way that the liquid wouldn't spill even when the jar was tipped over.

The Myceneans were known throughout the Mediterranean for their beautifully decorated pottery and other works of art like gold jewellery and seals made of precious stones. They copied this art from the Minoans who had the most developed civilization in the Aegean Sea. This wasn't the only thing they got from the Cretans as is the case when the people of a lesser developed civilization come into contact with those of a more highly developed civilization. But intelligence is also needed to know what to adopt from another civilization and adjust it

21

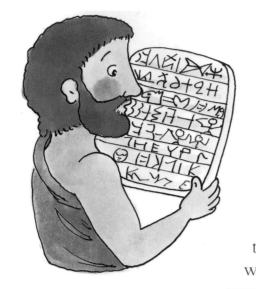

to the needs of your own. And the Myceneans, as Greeks, had plenty!

When the Cypriot ship left port it didn't take the usual route back to Cyprus which was by the coast line of Asia Minor. And this was not because they wanted to prevent anything terrible from happening, or because they feared the same route taken by the two unfortunate ships that had sunk a few months earlier. The reason was merely that the ship had to stop in Crete because the Mycenean king wanted to send a message to his older cousin who was king of Knossos. (The custom of kings from the central part of Greece being crowned in Crete started almost two hundred years before when the Myceneans, who had superior military power, conquered the Minoan part of Crete). So the ship had another five-day journey to Crete, and with favourable winds they hoped to be in Cyprus in another three days if the boat could sail at a speed of 8 to 10 knots.*

All the goods that were imported and exported from the port were written down in detail by the accountants and clerks of the palace. In one hand the clerk would hold the tablet, still soft because it had just been made out of clay. Making sure that the tablet wouldn't get wet from the rain, he carved with a pointed tool, numbers and other strange symbols that represented the names of the products, the quantity and the customers involved. When the tablet was filled in, the clerk would let it dry and then put it on special shelves in a row with other tablets. These were kept in a special room of the palace used for archives. The scribe was very responsible and proud of his job. Imagine that the king had once proclaimed this job a "ministry" rather than a position because only a few people in the whole kingdom knew how to read and write.

Life went on peacefully, full of activity, in the Mycenean palace for over 150 years. Of course there were some difficulties and problems. Once, the king left for ten years with the biggest part of his army and navy to go on a military campaign against Troy. Finally they conquered and destroyed the rival city that had control of the Straits which hadn't allowed the Myceneans to extend their

*Unit of speed used by ships – One nautical mile per hour. The coastal vesels which we travel to the islands with, sail at a speed of about 15-20 knots.

trade to the area of the Black Sea.

There was another time when the occupants of the palace had to abandon their quarters for over two months because of a fire which had burnt the interior. No one ever found out who did it and why. Some said that it had started from the hearth in the chamber where the throne was. Others claimed that the fat queen-mother had turned over the oil lamp. And the "shrewder" people said that it was deliberately started by the supporters of the envious brother of the king. Luckily only the rugs, furniture and curtains were burnt. They managed to put the fire out before it burnt the doors and the wooden beams of the roof.

The repairs were done quickly but it seems that this crisis was a curse and from then on things went from bad to worse in the kingdom. Business wasn't going well and the people became poor and miserable. And as if that wasn't enough, a rumour started that some fierce enemies were coming down from the North and were destroying everything in their path. The young, inexperienced king was terrified. So he took his family –his widowed mother, wife and children– and some of his closest aids and secretly took a boat to the East. They were going to go live in Miletus in Asia Minor, where they had a friend. He was a king in that area and although they didn't know him personally, they had corresponded in matters of trade and had exchanged gifts twice. So, he welcomed them and offered them hospitality.

However, the fierce enemy from the North never came down as far as the kingdom and the palace. They had changed direction. But the abandoned palace remained deserted and gradually deteriorated from the rain, snow and heat. Finally, not too much later, it collapsed and became ruins burying with it the remains of a great civilization. And so, the hill got bigger and bigger...

BUILDING

Activity in the area had never stopped. The village in the plains continued to exist for a long time with its old, closed agricultural society and economy and the memories of the great Mycenean past seemed like a fairy tale. The inhabitants were very industrious and creative and were soon involved in activities such as trade and shipping. As a result of this rapid development the village turned into a prosperous city once more.

Although the great palace of the past had been deserted, the walls of the Mycenean acropolis were intact. That was how well they were built. At some time, however, many years later, the inhabitants of the city tore them down and transported the stones to the river. They then built dams and fortified the banks of the river in order to prevent another disaster that had happened the past winter.

After a very heavy rain that kept up for three days, the river overflowed and flooded all the fields destroying the labour of an entire year.

The ruins of the acropolis and the palace that were left made the hill even higher at that spot. And so, after a few centuries, around 500 B.C. the people wanted to rebuild a big temple in honour of their beloved goddess, Athena. Without a second thought they chose that same spot; not only because it was the highest and most impressive area in the surrounding plains, but also because of the myths and tales that the older people sang about. These songs talked about the mythical kings of the territory whose roots went back to the great heroes and further back to the gods of Olympus.

Now, building a temple in ancient times wasn't an easy task. There was a certain democratic procedure to be followed which many Greek cities had started to adopt some years before. This change had stirred up great enthusiasm and desire for creativity by the citizens as it allowed them to take part in the system of decision making. This included their ability to elect and keep a check on their leaders. All the citizens gathered together about once a month at the "assembly of the people" and made decisions on every topic, big or small. And moreover, these decisions were made by the rich and the poor,

THE GREAT TEMPLE

the sailors and the artists, the painters and the coal makers. The only ones that complained were some old land owners because, they said, they lost their privileges. Also, protests were once heard by a group of women who had been educated and, as it was said, whose "minds had opened up to demand political rights". But the men just laughed with these goings-on because they didn't consider the women to be equal and worthy of taking part in public activities. Better for them to be closed up at home to spin and weave!

Anyway, what is significant is that at the last assembly of the people, a proposal was put forward to rebuild the great temple. This was voted on and passed by the majority of the people, despite the protests of the opposition party. A five-member committee was set up to oversee the project and handle the finances. The people that were responsible for this quickly drew up the plans which included the size of the temple, its style, the number of columns, the material, the design of the roof and doors, and anything pertaining to the sculptured decoration on the pediments of the building. When all of this was written on a plaque, the architects interested in taking on the project were invited to see the plans. Only three appeared as the others were afraid they couldn't take on such a difficult project. Meanwhile, rumour had it that the project had already been given to the most famous architect of the city, which happened to be the king's friend, and that the competition for the project was held anyway just to keep up appearances.

The three other architects decided to take the plans anyway and work them out with their colleagues. So each architect made detailed plans of the entire temple, estimated the cost of the materials and how much to pay the constructors (architects, quarry men, transporters, stone cutters, builders, wood carvers, painters, sculptors, etc.). This was included in their estimate of the total cost and how much time it would take to complete the project. They also made a model, a miniature temple, on a scale of 1:100 so the committee could decide on the final plan of the building.

After the plans were handed in, the committee met to judge the best one.

Without much thought, they decided to give the construction of the temple to the great architect of the city. Even his competitors admitted that he had drawn up the best plans, had the cheapest cost, and guaranteed the earliest deadline for the completion of the building. While the contract was being signed the committee reminded the architect of the law that had been passed the year before –that every architect or contractor that undertook any public construction had to put down his own property as a guarantee. The state had the right to bind that property and if the final cost of the construction went over the estimate by one fourth, it had the right to confiscate his property depending on how much over the estimate it was.

The day after the contract was signed, the project got under way. They started by hiring the needed workforce. Artists and workers came not only from the city, but also from far away. They had found out about the big project and the excellent wages being offered. A lot of slaves were also taken on, especially the stronger slaves for the heavier work. From the very beginning they ordered to quarries to start cutting the stones needed for the building. They would use porous rock for the base and marble for the rest of the building. They also gave an engineer orders to construct a crane and other small machines necessary for building.

Four years had almost gone by since the building started and everyone was pleased with the pace. Levelling the area and building the supporting walls didn't take long at all. It took longer time, more work and money to lay the foundations of the temple. It was next to these foundations where the priest saughtered a rooster as a symbol of "firm foundations" for the building. Everyone present, workers and officials alike, were taken aback to see the rooster put up such a fight and kick so much before he was sacrificed. For the more superstitious people this was not a good omen.

Next came the setting up of the drums* of the columns. But because the crane

* a drum is one of the cylindrical blocks which make up the shaft of the column

was new and they didn't know how to use it properly, a drum slid off the rope and injured two workers' feet. Immediately the other workers went on strike demanding that measures be taken for their protection against construction accidents. In the end everything worked out and the building began again after a delay of two weeks.

The construction work was very organized. Everyone was a specialist in his field of work and there was excellent cooperation in the quarries, in the transporting of materials and on the construction site. Big carts pulled by four or eight pairs of oxen or mules carried the huge cylindrical stones which the younger stone carvers then took charge of. They roughly carved the surface of each cylindrical stone leaving four bulky extensions on the sides forming something like an "elbow". To these "elbows" they tied the thick ropes which were attached to the cranes that lifted the huge stones. The drums of the columns were set up unfinished. The procedure of carving the flutes of the columns was done by a special team of workers made up of the best carvers. They began carving when the capital of the column was put in position.

Everyone, from the higher ranks to the last worker, was pleased with the progress of the project and they all did their best. This temple was to be a glorification of their city and its people. But luck and the historical circumstances were not on their side. Before the temple was finished and the idol was set up for worshipping, enemies invaded the city burning the people's houses and belongings. The wood and scaffolding of the temple also caught fire damaging the columns, the walls and the floor. Those who fled the city returned a few days after the enemy left only to find the city and the brilliant white temple turned into a pile of black ruins. And so, the hill got bigger and bigger...

THE SPLENDID CITY

The continuous wars in the mainland of Greece caused many difficulties and problems. They were either civil wars between the city-states which Greece was then divided into, or later wars between Hellenistic leaders and the Romans. Despite this, life in the city continued and the citizens took advantage of the wealth their developed civilization had to offer.

Their city was filled with beautiful public buildings and all hours of the day it bustled with life and activity. The temple had been rebuilt a few years earlier. It stood on the foundations of the old one, but now it was different. It had an Ionian design with many architectural sculptures, carved decorations and impressive ornamental drawings. The citizens were faithful in performing their religious duties regularly, participating in all the ceremonies and worship related to the gods of Olympus. They went to the sanctuaries with their families, where they gathered around the altar outside the main entrance of the temple to attend the sacrificial rite. When the priest finished, his assistants cut up the animals and roasted them. All the faithful chanted with their hands lifted towards the sky where the smoke was going up. However, some of them were easily carried away by the aroma of the roasting meat and threw furtive glances at what the priest would soon divide among them. The "common mortals" had to wait in line for a long time for their turn to come. The first ones to get the meat were the "aeisitoi", that is, those who were nourished in the Prytaneum after a decision made by the city government. Included in this privileged group were the nobility, those who had made large donations to the city and of course the Olympic Game champions who received great honour for their country.

On this particular day there was also a trade fair going on near the temple. The porticos, the fountains and the public buildings that surrounded the trade fair were ringing with people's voices and discussions. The native craftsmen

OF THE CLASSICAL ERA

and merchants had opened up their shops early in the portico and were selling furniture, cooking utensils, clay pots and various other things. On the top floor of the portico some of the shops sold products solely for the faithful who wanted to make an offering to the temple. These items included small clay idols of animals, beautiful multi-coloured clay vases and, for the wealthier people, gold or silver offerings.

The children liked gathering on the top floor of the portico because here, merchants were selling some beautiful little clay dolls called "plagones" and other dolls which moved their hands and feet, called marionettes. From here the children could also see the action in the market place and watch the religious processions which passed through the portico. The other activities they enjoyed watching were the cock fights, foreign acrobats, sword swallowers and other magicians with their fascinating tricks.

In the middle of the market where there was more space and cool shade under the trees, the farm producers had set up their booths very early and displayed what they had brought to the city with their carriages –fresh vegetables and fruit, chickens, eggs, small pigs and calves. Shorty after, a weary mule arrived from the sea pulling a cart with fresh oysters and red mullet. The fisherman bellowed that they were from the Aixonides Halai (what

is today Voula and Glyfada, seaside suburbs of Athens). When the fisherman's voice was heard, a group of men who had been absorbed by someone's improvised speech, broke up, to the speakers great disappointment, and ran to buy what their wives had asked them to. The wives themselves couldn't come to the market place because it was considered improper. So they would send their husbands or slaves to do the shopping. On the other hand, the women, especially the younger ones, were delighted with the chore of going to the public spring to fill their clay water vases. (They didn't have running water in their houses back then). Even thought the chore was tiring, especially if their house was far from the spring, the visit to the spring was a favourite activity because it gave the women a chance to make a public appearance; and perhaps a chance to exchange stolen glances with a young man.

Meanwhile a ship had come into port from the East with an impressive figurehead in the shape of a bird which had drawn the attention of many children who came down to the quay to look at it. The ship had brought papyrus from Egypt to cover the needs of the schools and the public and private libraries of the city. Available for sale were also precious perfumes and a beautiful delicate fabrics from a material called cotton. These fabrics were especially appealing for the rich ladies and maidens of the city because the native cloth which was made out of wool and linen was too rough for their delicate velvety skin. The imported cloth was a bit expensive, not only, because the shrewd traders wanted a good profit, but also because of taxes imposed by the port authorities. However, the women thought it was worth the money so they could make their grand appearance at the next Thesmophoria*.

In one of the buildings of the market place there was usually a queue of foreign traders, mostly. In this building sat the money-changers, that is, the people in charge of exchanging currency. They had their currency spread out on square wooden tables, ("trapeza", which means "table" or "bank" in Greek), and that's where the transactions took place. They couldn't possibly imagine

* Thesmophoria: a religious celebration in honour of the goddess Demetra where only women took part.

that after many thousands of years the banks of our modern times would take on this name ("trapeza" or "bank").

With the religious celebration of the great feast of the city, the inhabitants and visitors had the opportunity to enjoy two significant events. The first was theatrical performances of both tragedies and comedies. They had to queue for a long time in front of two huts outside the theatre to get their tickets which was a lead symbol with the head of the goddess Athena. The second event was the athletic races which took place in the stadium. It was easier to find tickets here, although this year attendance was higher than four years ago because everyone wanted to see the two famous athletes from Locroi and Taras in Southern Italy. This was the first time they were taking part in the competition, the first in wrestling and the other in the pentathlon (a five-event competition).

In the market place around the temple and in other important places marble and bronze statues were erected. They were either gods, or various mortals whom the city had honoured for their services and contributions. The tallest statue was the one of the Winged Victory in honour of the victory of the soldiers over the warring neighbouring city. But the most impressive statue was that of a warrior, "the old general", as he was called. His name had been inscribed on the tall base of the statue, but it had also gone down in the history of the city.

Just recently, in the little free space in the centre of the city a new building was constructed where all the boys gathered to train and exercise their bodies under the guidance of a gymnastics teacher. It was essential to maintain good physical condition so that a few years later they would become good soldiers. At the same time, the boys received a general education which helped them to become good conscious citizens, combining the virtues of "sound body and soul".

THE GREAT

In spite of the Roman conquest, life in the city during the first Christian centuries went on basically at the same pace. People saw the differences from the old times but really didn't pay to much attention to it. Only the more "sensitive" citizens were angry that the ancestral form of government operated in name only. They didn't like the fact that the most competent, or at least, popular, candidates were not getting into office, but rather, that the rich were buying their way into government positions. And this was an accepted, even established way of doing things. But then, the authority of the local leaders had diminished over the years, limited to trivial everyday problems of management, whereas the major decisions of government were made in Rome. This, however, was no excuse for the way elections were taking place where there was not even a pretext of voting rules.

The presence of the Romans had left its mark on the city. For example, many statues next to the temple were missing, leaving only their bases with the inscriptions on them. And that was because the Roman generals and emperors that had passed through established the custom of taking some of the statues with them, preferably the bronze ones, to add to their loot and decorate the public and private buildings of their capitals.

The worst damage was done by Nero. This mad emperor,considering himself to be the greatest actor, musician and athlete, abandoned Rome and the governing of the state. He then made his rounds to all the Greek cities and large temples "winning" all the musical, theatrical and athletic competitions. Along with the loot he loaded on his boats was the famous statue of the "Winged Victory" and the "Old General". The inhabitants were very sad to see their city being stripped, especially when the "Old General" was taken. They felt as if they'd lost an old friend and protector.

Other changes were made, too. The orchestra of the theatre, where the chorus stood in earlier times in the theatrical performances, was turned into an arena

DISASTER

for wild animal fights. Some people had even reached the point of turning the theatre into a lake so they could simulate naval battles with miniature boats, a game that had become very popular at the time.

Despite all this, the city continued to honour and flatter not only the emperors, but many lesser officers as well. The most common way of doing this was to erect honorary statues in the market place. But because times were difficult and the city finances were limited, they would honour the person by replacing only the heads of the older statues and the inscriptions on the bases. That way everyone was satisfied.

By now many people had become fed up with the political situation and moral decline. Coupled with this was the slackening in the belief in the ancient gods. So they started searching for other virtues. Some resorted to the belief in Egyptian or Persian gods like Isis or Mithras. But others began to believe in something totally new. A community was created made up of people called Christians who believed in some "Christ" who had preached a new religion a few years earlier in Palestine. However, he had been sentenced to death by the Romans and Jews. One of Christ's disciples named Paul, had come to the city to talk about Christ's teachings. The first time he came, there were only a few people who gathered to listen to him. But slowly the faithful grew in number and communities became larger and more organized. This began to worry the Roman rulers.

But that wasn't the most threatening thing for the peaceful law-abiding citizens. Rumour had it that hordes of Germanic tribes with strange names like Herulians and Goths, were coming down from the north spreading calamity and destruction. The news seemed to have disturbed the emperor as he issued an edict that ordered the local administrators and citizens to immediately repair the city walls and everything else needed to fortify the city.

Everyone heeded the orders of the emperor and work started immediately. They worked fast under a lot of pressure. They needed easy building material, so they didn't hesitate to tear down an abandoned temple near the walls. Even the tombstones from the graves at the cemetery right outside the city were torn apart. Panic had taken over as everyone felt the oncoming danger and shivered to think about what could happen to them. There was great concern over the fact that most of the men had become "soft". That is, they had never held a weapon in their lives. And only a few, some emancipated slaves and veteran soldiers in the city, could organize and lead the defence.

And so it happened. They had just finished temporarily repairing the walls and had taken up their weapons when a black line appeared in the distance. Dust stirred up from the trampling horses of the enemy as they approached the city. The soldiers were outnumbered by the enemy so they didn't have any difficulty getting into the city. After that the scene was indescribable. First they killed everyone they saw in front of them. After that they went into the houses and murdered the women and children. Their wrath was so great that the only ones who managed to escape were those who found shelter on a ship that had just docked at the port. The barbarians didn't even hesitate to go in the temple and desecrate the statue. Laughing, they knocked it off its base and set fire to it. The goddess' clothes caught on fire immediately and the fire spread to the red carpet that covered the floor. From there it quickly spread to the wooden roof whose thick beams of cypress wood became an easy prey for the burning tongues of fire. Suddenly creaking was heard and afterwards there was a terrible sound accompanied by a cloud of dust. The roof of the temple collapsed, taking with it parts of the wall and the supporting columns.

The fire continued to spread to the adjoining porticos of the market-place burning the wooden doors of the shops. In no time the large jars filled with oil that were stored in the merchants shops caught on fire. The flames were fierce here because of the highly flammable material, and the sound was frightening as the tongues of fire reached into the sky. After that it wasn't difficult for the gymnasium and the rest of the houses to catch on fire. A little further down some maniacs tried to set fire to the theatre and stadium, but they didn't succeed. By now the sky had darkened from the smoke and ashes. Never had such a disaster occurred in the city!

The burying of the dead was the first concern for the few that survived. There were so many dead and the danger of disease so great that the only immediate solution was to put aside the ancestral laws of burying the dead and throw them in deep trenches, covering them with ample dirt so they would be safe from the dogs. And so they were buried all together the rich and the poor, the young and the old, men, women and children. Where were the old times of peace, where one was buried alone in a private grave in his family enclosure in the cemetery outside the city wall? Where were the exquisite pieces of art, sculptures or vases which were placed either on, or in the graves depicting the social status of the dead? Now, not a single tombstone could be found to put on the top of the graves!

THE TEMPLE BECOMES

About two hundred years had gone by, but the next generations of the inhabitants that survived the catastrophe of the great ancient city had not forgotten what happened. There was a place just outside the village where many bones had been found. This, they called "The Bones" because they believed this was where the slaughter had taken place. A little further away was a huge rock which had a natural reddish colour, but the villagers believed its colour had come from their ancestors' blood. So they named it "The Bloody Rock". They could see the scattered ruins of the ancient city and knew that they were living on the site of what was once a great thriving civilization.

Life went on, and around the end of the fifth century A.D. the people thought about building a large church. Christianity had become widespread and was the official religion of the state. There was no longer any reason for Christians to gather secretly in order to practice their religion. But the village was poor and there was no money for the building of a big new church. They could, however, get permission from the emperor of Constantinople who allowed the reconstruction of abandoned ancient temples for communities who couldn't afford to build new places of worship.

After getting the approval of the local bishop, the people began rebuilding the ancient temple to make it a church. What was left of the temple was in terrible condition. The fire had damaged the monument beyond repair, but since then the rain, the ice and the snow had completed the destruction. Besides, the temple had become a favourite playground, because it was the highest point in the village. There, on the marble steps, the children wrote or carved various games using coal.

With the leadership of their priest, the faithful worked in groups in order to get the building of the new church underway. People didn't get paid for their work, but rather, felt it was their obligation. Each person would give up an entire workday to give of their services to community work as they had done

A CHURCH

a few years earlier when they repaired the bridge.
The first thing they did was to clear the stones and dirt from the interior of the temple. They carefully took apart the walls and with the same stones they filled the gaps between the columns that were left. This way, the interior became larger and there would be ample room for all the faithful. They also divided the interior with two rows of columns to support the wooden rafters of the roof. This way they could make the women's quarters on the upper floor of the side aisles. Other changes also had to be made because of the difference in orientation between the Christian churches and the ancient temples. On the narrow east side where the entrance of the ancient temple had been, they now built the apse for the sanctuary. The main entrance was opposite this, on the west side, although most of the people used a smaller entrance right in front of them as they walked up the sloping side. As an altar table they used a huge ancient plaque with an inscription on it which they found outside the temple. This they laid on the capital of a column to form a table.

They had to get the bishop's permission to do all this. He also told them to carve big crosses on the ancient architectural parts to expel any "spirits" of the pagan religion which might still be embedded in the stone. The back chamber of the temple was transformed into the narthex of the church and outside, in the churchyard, a circular font was constructed by placing an ancient marble vessel for lustral water on top of a small pillar.

The floor of the church was funded by a rich fellow citizen. A famous mosaic expert was brought in from Antioch to decorate the floor with beautiful marble and mosaics. He worked with his assistants for three months and when the work was finished and the floor was wiped down, everyone was enthused with the results.

When the mosaic workers finished, the sculptors began placing on the iconostas the beautifully carved marble panels depicting a vase with flowers between two peacocks. These had been previously carved in a special workshop by the sculptors.

The final stage was fixing the roof and everything was then ready for the celebration of the grand opening. The iconography was to be done later on when they had gathered enough money to pay a good iconographer who, with his assistants, travelled around Greece to do this work.

The ceremony of the consecration was done of course by the bishop who was to bring the icon of the saint to whom the church would be dedicated. After a long, and somewhat tiring liturgy, the bishop signalled the congregation to join in the chanting of "Glory to God in the Highest". At this moment he lifted up the new icon of the Virgin Mary which would be venerated from now on in the church.

Everyone was pleased that things had turned out this way. They liked the fact that the new church had been built on the site of the ancient temple. Although the ancient gods seemed so different now, the people still felt some ties to the past and couldn't completely ignore their existence. Many said that the reason the bishop dedicated the church to the Virgin Mary was because the goddess Athena had been worshipped in the ancient temple. But most of the faithful now believed that it was truly divine enlightenment of the Holy Spirit. Whatever the case, everyone seemed to be quite content with the change. They had heard in other places things hadn't gone so smoothly. Many fanatic Christians had raided the ancient religious temples and destroyed them completely. They knocked the statues off their bases and began breaking them with hammers and ruined many beautiful works of art with the purpose of eradicating any trace of the ancient religion.

A lot of time passed by since then and with all the trials and tribulations the

villagers didn't manage to get the iconography done in the church. Now, however, in the first half of the 11th century the time had come. A group of iconographers from Handaka, Crete were putting the finishing touches on a grouping of warrior saints on the walls of the side aisle of the church. The board members of the church were in a hurry for the work to be finished by the first Sunday of Lent, which fell on March 11 that year. They wanted this so that the iconography could be blessed on the same day as the great feast of the Sunday of Orthodoxy. This was a celebration of the reinstatement of icons in the churches after the iconoclastic conflict.

In the meantime the ships that were arriving from Constantinople were bringing news that things were not going very well there. There was a lot of gossip around the empress Zoe's third marriage to a soldier named Constantine Monomachos. People were angry with the waste of the puplic money by the palace for the licentious life and luxuries of the royal family and military aristocracy. Everyone was also troubled by the news from Asia Minor about the appearance of a new people, the Seljuk Turks. They were making their way towards the eastern borders of the empire with hostile intentions.

THE YEARS

The years went by fast and the historical events brought the village, as well as all the Byzantine empire, under Turkish domination. Times were hard. People worked in the fields and at other jobs feeling the heavy breath of their conqueror on their necks. However, the village was small and remote so the Turks that settled there were few and not cruel. They lived harmoniously with the enslaved Greeks; they had learned to speak Greek and lived together without much discrimination and continuous friction between conqueror and slave as was so in the larger cities. Greek and Turkish children played together and it wasn't easy to tell them apart. A mosque had even built in the middle of the village to meet the religious needs of the Turkish inhabitants.

The difficulties began when, twice a year, the Turkish tax collector showed up in the village. All the men had to present him with a record of what they had produced, with their hard labour, the previous tax period. The farmers had to declare how many animals had been born, the amount of flour produced and the vegetables that were grown. The stock-breeders reported the number of animals they fed or the milk and cheese they produced. Even the wine and honey from the beehives had to be declared. The tax collector then made his calculations and established what commodities each person had to deposit in the treasury. Of course this was usually much more than the amount of their profit. But, the people just bowed their heads with humility and anger and laid down the requested amount of commodity in front of the tax collector. They felt they had just given a whole part of their life, a part of their body!

It wasn't long before the inhabitants actually did give a part of their flesh. The sultan's decree had spread terror and panic among the enslaved Greeks. It declared that every Christian family had to give up a male child from 15 to 20 years old to be taken, with others, to special army camps to be trained according to the Ottoman discipline. They would then become part of a special

OF TURKISH DOMINATION

division of Turkish soldiers called janissaries. As the days for the gathering of young men approached the parents became despondent. The more daring ones were prepared to take their children and go hide in the mountain caves. Others dressed their sons up like girls to avoid the sacrifice, and others even declared they had changed their religion and become Moslems to save their families from this blood tax imposed by the conqueror.

The village slowly began to die out. The old people gradually passed away and the younger ones, as many as they could, left for the islands of the Ionian Sea and other areas occupied by the Venetians. Others found refuge on the Holy Mountain and became monks, while others went to hide in the mountains far away. So it wasn't long before the village was completely deserted. The roofs of the houses began collapsing and the walls afterwards. Grass began to grow on the deserted land and the fields became overrun by small bushes. It wasn't long before they became a thick forest.

The big church, deserted and no longer used for services, slowly began to deteriorate. Only a few Christians from the neighbouring village came every Saturday after vespers to light the vigil lamps in the ruins. Then, one night a blurred image of a woman appeared in a village woman's dream telling her to rebuild the church. This was a difficult, almost impossible task to accomplish. Besides, they weren't sure they would be able to get permission from the Turkish authorities to carry out such a large project. So they decided to build a small country church on top of the old ruins of the big church. The husband and two sons of the woman finished the work fast – in one week! There were plenty of stones from the ruins of the big church and assembling them was easy. But they had a difficult time finding some unbroken tiles among the ruins to fix the roof. When everything was finished the younger son, who knew how to read and write, carved a plaque which he fixed to the wall with these words: ΑΝΗΓΕΡΘΗ Ο ΝΑΟΣ ΟΥΤΟΣ ΜΗΝΙ ΙΟΥΛΙΩ ΕΤΕΙ ΑΨΛΖ*.

The woman who had the dream wanted something more. A long time ago she had found an engraved plaque half hidden in the dirt in one of the fields. When she cleaned it, it revealed the figure of a woman holding a child in her arms. This reminded her of the icons of the Virgin Mary with the Christ-child and she began venerating it without much thought. So now that the temple was built she asked her sons to transfer the heavy marble plaque there and place it next to a simple vigil light. Thus, the engraved tombstone of the 4th century B.C. which had been placed on the grave of an old woman and her grandchild was easily transformed into the icon of the Virgin Mary the Child-bearer.

Time went by, but the circumstances remained unchanged. There were, however, some Greeks who had emigrated abroad and became merchants. They were able to develop financially and set up large Greek communities that

never forgot their enslaved brothers whom they helped every way they could. But within the country, life was very difficult. That's why many young men, with the consent of their parents, fled to the mountains and became rebels. There they lived under very difficult conditions, especially in the winter, where they had to steal in order to survive. Slowly they developed the spirit of rebelliousness which was shown by their refusal to bow their head to the Turkish authorities.

There were others who supposedly came to terms with the Turks. In exchange for exemption from taxation and other obligations they set up armed forces which guarded the main routes and passages or important areas of the borders. And then there were many young men who went to sea, either willingly as crew members on merchant ships ot pirate ships, or unwillingly as oarsmen on the ships of the sultan's armada. All these men never lost their ethnic consciousness, keeping within them their zeal for freedom. When the time came, they were quick to join the powerful movement which led to the

*This temple was erected the month of July in the year 1737.

52

struggle for freedom.

This struggle would not have been possible if, during all these years of bondage, the enslaved generation hadn't been educated. This is what kept the ethnic and religious conscious of the Greeks alive. Disregarding the difficulties and dangers, more and more children walked for hours once a week to climb up to the monasteries or go to the larger cities where the communities had established the "schools of common and sacred letters": Here, either monks or teachers who had finished the school of higher learning, taught the Greek children to read, write and do arithmetic. But most of all the children liked listening to stories about the ancient Greeks: Hercules, Achilles, Odysseus, and later Themistocles, Pericles and Alexander the Great. The teachers also talked to them with great passion about Justinian the Bulgar-slayer and Constantine Paleologos. On hearing these stories the children felt very proud, but at the same time, were saddened when they compared these stories to what was going on then. However, a spark of hope was born in them that one day freedom would come and they would once more become a great significant nation as before.

THE EXCAVATION

One hundred and fifty years of freedom went by after the great Revolution of 1821. With this came prosperity, that is, the abundance of material goods, which gave Greeks and foreigners the opportunity to travel and enjoy the beauty of Greece's natural surroundings. With tourism, there was a need to construct large hotels and accomodations for the holiday makers. Unfortunately this also brought about trespassing of properties, makeshift houses and of course, a lot of litter. However, the land which nurtured so many generations and hosted so many different cultures continued to be beautiful. The mountains formed a magnificent background for the dark green colour of the forest. The river, even though shallow, wound its way through the hills and fields. The sea with its multi-coloured pebbles was an ideal place for swimming. Dominating the whole area was a large hill with a small church perched on top of it.

This hill was quite strange. It rose abruptly from the beach in such a way that really didn't fit in with the natural relief of the land. It had a peculiar shape, various chiseled stones were thrown here and there, and many pieces of broken pottery were scattered thoughout the area all the way down to the beach. A young archaeologist, who had come to the beach to swim with his family, took notice of all this.

He climbed up to the church and stood for a while in front of the door trying to decipher the inscription "MHNI IOYΛIΩ ETEI AΨΛZ" "the month of July in the year 1737." "Oh, we've got here a typical church from the second period of the Turkish occupation", he said to himself. "But what's this here?", he continued with surprise looking at a spot on the wall where the plaster had fallen off. "It's built with ancient marble stones! Then there should be a significant ancient building around, maybe a temple," he said.

Then he started walking around the hill carefully and gathered some pieces of

BEGINS ...

broken pottery that had been buried among the rocks and dry grass. Holding his "findings" in his hands he climbed back up to the church and sat down under the shade. He laid the pottery on the wall surrounding the church and started examining each one carefully. His face lit up. It was clear that the pieces dated back from ancient times all the way up to modern times. He immediately realized that the hill had been formed by the successive habitation and destruction layers of many settlements in the same area which lasted hundreds or even thousands of years. "If the strata of ruins are intact then we've got here a unique ancient treasure", he said to himself.

After a whole year of preparations, the excavation began at a fast pace. First of all, the archaeologists blocked out 5x5 metre squares on the surface of the hill next to the small church. Then before special technicians and workers began excavating, the archaeologists gathered them together and gave them basic instructions– they had to dig very carefuly and examine the dirt. They weren't allowed to pick up any stones or ancient ruins from the ground without having first photographed it and sketched it on paper. They also had to note any changes of colour and form that they found in the dirt and lastly, they had to be very careful not to mix up the findings of the different layers. They all had to be put in separate bags and labelled according to where each came from.

The technicians started digging carefully and shovelling the dirt onto small carts which were then emptied at the other end of the hill. In the beginning the dirt was soft and black from the roots of the grass and bushes, so the work went fast until they reached the depth of half a metre. There they discovered that the texture and colour of the dirt was different and it was very hard, full of bricks and lime. Shortly afterwards they same upon the collapsed walls. Under one of the walls that formed a small arch one could make out part of a wall painting depicting half of a saint's face. "Aha! Here we've got a large older Byzantine church", said the archaeologist. "It's not unusual for a small chapel to have been built on top ot an older church. At first glance the wall painting looks like it goes back to the mid-Byzantine era, the 11th or 12th century."

He then took a thick notebook, which is called a diary, and wrote down the depth of the excavation, the formation of the dirt the photographs of the findings and his remarks. After that it was the responsibility of the icon restorer to try to carefully detach the wallpainting. The draughtman's job was to sketch the lay-out and diagram of the excavation site, and the photographer's job was to take general shots from a tall ladder and detailed shots from up close.

After removing the dirt that covered the ancient ruins at about 1 1/2 metres from the surface, the floor of the church showed through in some spots and one could see the mosaics. "You must work very carefully here", said the archaeologist to the technicians. "At this depth, the excavation has to be carried out with a small broom so that no damage is done to the floor". The work continued extensively with the aim of exposing the entire mosaic floor. From the synthesis of the design and colours thcy wcrc able to date the floor back to the 5th century A.D. which was verified by the findings of the marble icon screen panels in the eastern section built in the same era. In one corner of the church on the floor, two metal oil lamps and three coins were found intact. The findings were labelled with a number, placed in separate bags and sent to the nearest museum workshop to be cleaned. These were very important findings because they were found on the floor and enabled the archaeologist to date the destruction and abandonment of the church. So he opened up his diary once again and carefully recorded everything in detail.

Excavation of each blocked out square continued gradually revealing the rest of the church floor. They found stones that had fallen from the walls, drums and capitals of columns from an ancient temple. Judging from the type and design of the capitals of the columns, the archaeologist was able to conclude that the temple was of Ionic style, probably built in the Hellenistic period. What really impressed the archaeologist, however, was the damage found on the marble interior of the temple as well as on the capitals of the columns. He had never come across anything like this and couldn't explain it. So he called in a friend, an archaeologist from the Department of Restoration and asked for his help. After carefully examining the damage he concluded that the marble and capitals had suffered "thermal breakage", that is, that the cracks were created by extremely high temperatures. "The ancient temple must have been destroyed by fire," he said at the end of the conversation. The other archaeologist was deep in thought trying to recall the disasters that had occurred in the city from what the ancient writers had mentioned. That way he would be able to tell which of the ruins dated back to which time.

From this point on the excavation stopped after three months of continuous hard work. Everyone was tired but very satisfied at the big celebration they had on their last night. They had gone through a lot with the sun and heat, the dirt and dust, and of course with the government which at one point didn't have enough money to pay the workers. In spite of all this, they had done a good job as the various visiting archaeologists to the site had all admitted.

The next day, before departing from the excavation site, the technicians and workers had to make sure the ruins would be protected and preserved. They made a big shelter which covered the ruins of the church and the ancient temple, giving special attention to preserving the mosaics. At the same time, in the storeroom of the excavation site, they cleaned and glued pieces of ruins, sketched them and photographed the findings–clay vessels, marble sculptures, copper coins and other remains.

All this information would be used by the archaeologist during the winter where his work would continue in the city library. He would have to read many books, both Greek and foreign, about similar excavations in order to compare his findings to others which had previously been studied and dated. Then he would compare the notes in his diary to the conclusions from the studies, so that he could write up his article on the excavation that would be published by the official periodical of the Department of Antiquities which contained similar articles on excavations of that particular year.

... THE SECRETS

The following summer the excavation began again with the same skilled workers in addition to two students from the Department of Antiquities as assistants. Firstly, the area was cleared of grass and dirt so they could choose the specific site where they would continue their research. The excavation in the interior of the temple had been completed since they had unearthed a fixed floor. If they wanted to research the layers underneath this level, they would have to go to another part of the hill. They chose an area right outside the temple next to one of the pedestals so they could examine the foundations. The archaeologist roped off another 5x5 square and told the skilled technician to start digging. "Try to find the foundation ditch of the temple and collect all the findings so we can determine the specific period of construction", said the archaeologist.

The foundations were 3,5 metres deep from the surface, since they had to support such a large structure. Suddenly, right next to the foundation stones, the technician found a small pit with black fine oily dirt which clearly indicated decomposed living matter. He took a fine brush and began whisking the dirt away carefully until he came upon the fine bones of a bird. He enthusiastically called over the archaeologist who was, at the time, giving a guided tour to some primary school children. "Obviously it's from a foundation sacrifice. They probably killed a rooster and placed it here".

"But we're also talking about a custom that is practiced even today in the villages," added the technician.

The foundations went deeper passing down to a layer of light brown dirt with a lot of stones and pottery which dated back mainly to the Mycenean period. Thus the layer underneath was from the same period. But, because the strata at this point was broken down, the archaeologist decided to expand the excavation further away from the temple, towards the slope, hoping that the

ARE REVEALED

strata underneath would be intact. They roped off a square area and began working as usual from the surface. After digging for four days, at a depth of 1,5 metres they found part of a pedestal and two bases of a pillar from a portico. Between the bases was the bottom part of an inscribed plaque. Inscriptions are some of the most interesting and exciting findings of an excavation, since written texts are direct and clear evidence, for a specific area. Very often they are the only source for finding out the name of a city, or to which god a certain temple was dedicated. So the archaeologist bent over the plaque trying to clean the letters so he could read the inscription. However, it was quite worn away and the only thing he could decipher was the last phrase: ΕΝ ΑΓΟΡΑ ΣΤΗΣΑΙ*.

"If this plaque hasn't been transferred here from somewhere else, then the temple at the top of the hill must have been built beside, or in, the market place of a city", the archaeologist thought. "If that's so, then the houses and public buildings should be at the base of the hill and down in the plain next to the river", he continued.

But, as the excavation continued and interest had come to a peak, they had to stop working because the archaeologist and his team were called away for an "emergency excavation". In the neighbouring city three graves of the Hellenistic period were discovered in a ditch of the water company! When they returned after a two-week absence it took a couple of days to get back into the routine. The excavation had reached a depth of 4,2 metres where for

*ERECTED IN THE MARKET PLACE.

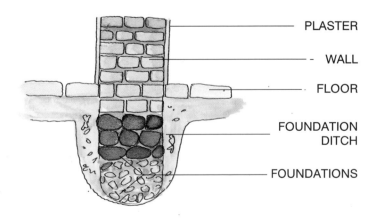

PLASTER

WALL

FLOOR

FOUNDATION DITCH

FOUNDATIONS

the first time, a clean layer 30cm thick was discovered without any findings. The archaeologist concluded that the area had probably been abandoned for a period of time, but he could't say if this was limited to this particular spot or if it was the same for the rest of the hill. A little further down, however, they discovered, again, the upper surface of the light brown layer with the Mycenean pottery that they were looking for. It was clean and intact! They began work so intensely in the deep square hole and they were so involved, that they didn't even notice a group of tourists in their bathing suits who had climbed up and were watching the excavation with great interest.

The Mycenean layer had been uncovered throughout the large square and digging through it had just begun. But as one of the technicians was digging up an interior wall of a room in the corner of the square and distracted by one of the tourists in a bikini, a loud crack was heard. Everyone froze as that meant that his pick had just broken something. The archaeologist, who was studying the strata in the dug out section, jumped over to the corner and started brushing away the dirt. "It's impossible!" he shouted with mixed emotions. "A clay tablet with Linear B script! You just broke a clay tablet with Linear B script!" he screamed at the technician. "Don't worry", the technician answered calmly, "there are more underneath". The archaeologist looked at him full of surprise and started brushing away fervently. And sure enough quite a number of similar tablets came up. He couldn't hide his enthusiasm. "Not even Blegen was this lucky!" shouted the archaeologist overwhelmed by the findings. "The tablets mean we find ourselves in the archives of a Mycenean palace", he said later to the people sitting around him. He imagined himself sitting in the throne room, just as Agamemnon did, enjoying the authoritative power of his position over his subordinates.

It is neither easy nor common to find and unearth a Mycenean palace. The archaeologist saw the difficulties and problems that he faced every day especially with dating the clay pots. So he asked for help from an Englilsh colleague who had just done his doctorate's thesis on Mycenean pottery at the University of Cambridge. He felt more confident with his colleague's cooperation. The excavation had to be done at a slower pace now because the archaeological strata were thinner and more frequent. So the differences in the clay pots, and of course the time period which they represented, were shorter. It was evident that one of the layers had come from the clearing of an area after a fire. The dirt was fine and ash-coloured and contained many pieces of coal. Also all the findings –pieces of wall paintings, clay pots, metal and bone jewellery– had obvious traces of having been on fire. "This layer is very interesting", said the Englishman. "It shows us that there was a fire just as in Mycenae, which dates back to the Mycenean IIIB period. However, it shouldn't have anything to do with the abandonment of the palace and the end of the Mycenean civilization which followed about a century later", he thought out loud.

In order to check out how far the palace extended, the archaeologists decided to dig in a new area, not high up at the top of the hill, but lower in the south side just where a road had cut into the slope. As it was, they could discern walls and floors where the road had cut into the side of the hill. This verified that the area was a continuation of the settlement. When the square area was roped off and the excavation progressed, they discovered that on this side of

the hill the strata were like the others. In the higher layers were remains of a Byzantine village. Further down were the lower layers of the Mycenean period. A little deeper however, at 5.8 metres, something quite interesting awaited them. There was a thick layer of the Neolithic period which up to now, had never been uncovered in the excavation site, as they had never dug down this far.

The first thing that was uncovered was the corner of a house formed by two walls, 40cm thick, built with small flat stones and mud. The floor was made of hard dirt, but most of it was covered by melted bricks. As soon as these were removed two flat stones were found, probably used as bases for wooden columns which supported the roof. The floor was full of fish bones, sea shells, animal bones and other remains of food, all mixed in with broken clay pots. "It seems that the housewives of the period didn't sweep their houses", the technician said jokingly. "That's how it usually was in the houses of the Neolithic period", answered the archaeologist. "Instead of cleaning the floors, they just covered them with a new layer of dirt. That's why the Neolithic layers are usually quite thick and consist of a succession of layers".

In one corner of the room they found a pebble carved into a human shape, two stone axes, blades made out of obsidian and a clay handmade bowl broken into many pieces. They immediately concluded that these items must have fallen from a shelf or niche on the wall. Suddenly, as a technician was carefully removing a mass of melted bricks, the end piece of a human bone showed through. "Come quickly", he called. The archaeologist stooped down, took the tools in his hands and continued digging himself. Shortly, the whole skeleton was uncovered. "In seems, from his position and the fact that he was buried underneath a brick wall, that he was killed when the house collapsed, probably from an earthquake", he thought. That afternoon he would call in the specialist from the medical school who studies ancient bones to take on the research. He could not only find out the sex and age of the skeleton, but also what illnesses he had gone through, what he ate and more.

In another part of the house, probably the courtyard, a pile of pebbles from the sea with holes in them were found. "Tell me", said the archaeologist to his colleague, "what do you think these were, weights from fish nets or parts of a loom? " He didn't have time to answer as a technician interrupted the conversation to announce that they had just found a layer of sand in another part of the courtyard. "I think we're heading for the end", said the archaeologist. "This layer of sand is probably where it all started".

So the excavation slowly came to an end. Everyone felt it had reached its goal. The hill had generously revealed its hidden secrets. But who knows. Maybe it had kept some secrets for itself!

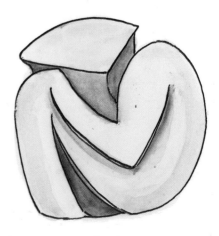

ACTIVITY SECTION

FROM THE CAVE ERA TO

1.   You too, can make handprints. You'll need a piece of cardboard, a straw and coloured chalk which has been ground to a fine dust. Wipe the cardboard with a wet cloth and fill the straws with the chalk dust. Place your palm on the wet cardboard and carefully blow out the chalk dust onto the area around your hand and in between your fingers. When it dries you'll have a handprint similar to the ones the prehistoric people made.

2.   Make a botanical collection. Gather some twigs of oregano, thyme, sage, lime flowers, mint, marjoram, etc. Pick off the leaves and put them in between pages of newspapers. Place heavy books or other objects on top of the newspapers and leave it like this for a week. When the leaves have dried, glue them to the pages of a scrapbook and label each herb.

3.   Find a small flower pot and fill it with dirt. Plant some grains of wheat and water them a little every three days. You'll soon see them sprout!

TO THE NEOLITHIC REVOLUTION

4.   Make stone tools. Collect flat pebbles from the beach and shape them into tools by striking them with another pebble.

5.   Find some sea shells, or small rocks which have natural holes in them, or small soft seeds which look like beads. Using a needle and strong thread, string them onto the thread to make a prehistoric necklace.

6.   You can sew clothes for your dolls like the clothes the prehistoric people made.

a. Cut two pieces of fabric like the pattern (illus. 1).

b. Sew the two pieces together and turn the pants right side out. Put them on your doll and tie them to the waist, with a string or ribbon (illus. 2). Make the blouse the same way using the pattern in (illus. 3). You'll need help from an adult.

(illus. 2)

(illus. 1)

(illus. 3)

A NEW BEGINNING

1.   How many of the activities described in this chapter can you find in the illustration on pages 12-13?

2.   Make a loom. You'll need 4 sticks and string to make the frame, and two different colours of yarn to weave with. Assemble the frame like the illustration. Tightly wrap one ball of yarn around the top and bottom sticks filling the frame from side to side. Take the other ball of yarn and fasten it firmly to one side. Weave the yarn in and out between the verticle strings of yarn. Do this until the loom fills up.

3. Take some clay and make a pot. Let it dry well in the sun or bake it in the oven. When it's ready, paint it with fingerpaint or watercolours.

AT THE NEOLITHIC SETTLEMENT

4. Take some hard sticks, rocks and heavy string and try making some prehistoric tools like the ones in the illustration.

5. What kind of bread did these people eat? Was it similar to what we eat today? Try making your own and note your observations. Here's what you'll need: all-purpose flour, salt and water. Place the flour and salt in a bowl and slowly add enough water to make a medium soft dough that doesn't stick to your hands. Knead well and shape into a square loaf. Place in a greased loaf pan and bake in preheated oven until it is brown on top. You'll need the help of an adult for this.

FLOUR   SALT   WATER

CASTLES AND PALACES

1. A jar with an unusual shape and name: the false-spouted stirrup jar. The aromatic oils would not spill out when this jar tipped over.

Which one is it? ....

A	B	C	D

Finish drawing the false-spouted stirrup jar.

2. I'm a .... I'll copy the script on clay.

IN THE MYCENEAN ERA

3.   Group games. Prepare an offering (at home) for the goddess. It can be a cake, cheese tarts, or anything else that can be eaten easily. Take your friends and line up in a procession, each one holding his offering. After placing the offerings on the altar of the goddess you can share your offerings with the others and enjoy eating them.

4.   Theatrical group game: Trade in the Mycenean cities:
Roles: a king, craftsmen, merchants.
The king bargains with the merchants on the price of the raw materials. He then gives them to his craftsmen to produce the goods. When they are ready, the king discusses the sales price and the quantity of goods with the merchants.

BUILDING

1. It took a lot of craftsmen and workers to build the great temple. Look closely at the large illustration at the beginning of the chapter.

a. How many different specialized workers do you see?

b. What kind of vehicles did they use to transport materials?

c. What do we call the mechanism that lifts the huge pieces of marble and helps put them in place?

d. How many different kinds of tools do they use?

The sculptor: .... and ....

The engineers .... and ....

The stone masons .... and ....

2. Make a crane like the one in the illustration. You'll need 3 sticks, 2 pulleys, rope and a hook.

THE GREAT TEMPLE

3.   Group game: Each person can design a plan for the building of an ancient temple and submit it to the "assembly of the people". With this plan you should also submit an estimate of the cost and a deadline for finishing the construction. The "assembly of the people" will decide which is the best offer.

4.   Group game: With the help of your teacher, organize an "assembly of the people" and decide on your next class excursion.

THE SPLENDID CITY

1.   Look closely at the illustration at the beginning of the chapter. Find the public buildings of the city. ....

....

2.   Make a puppet out of cardboard or clay. You'll find the model on page 34. If you make it out of cardboard you'll need to connect the arms and legs. If you make it out of clay, you'll need thin wire to pass through the arms and legs and connect them to the body while the clay is still wet.

3.   Theatrical game: Set up a market place where each "merchant" will try to attract customers by calling out why his wares are the best.

OF THE CLASSICAL ERA

4.   Look in other books and try to find plans or illustrations of ancient public buildings like temples, porticos, springs, theatres, stadiums or gymnasiums. You can find some related titles of books in the bibliography and the end of this book.

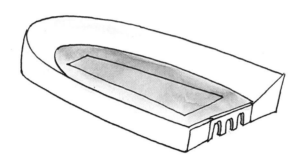

THE GREAT DISASTER

1.   Ancient cities faced danger from:

a.   Human factors like: ....

b.   Natural disasters like: ....

2. Group game: Each child brings a photograph of himself to the group. Cut the heads off the photographs and exchange heads placing them on the bodies of other children's photographs. This is what the Greeks did with their statues in the Roman times, if you remember.

3.   From whatever history you have learned, note down other times in the past when people have destroyed great civilizations.

....

....

THE TEMPLE BECOMES A CHURCH

1.   What do we call the period of history where the temple was rebuilt into a Christian church? ....

2.   How many fragments of ancient architecture do you see that were used in the new church? ....

3.   Make your own candles. In the Byzantine period there was no electricity and homes were lit up with candles. To make your own candles you'll need: string, a small stick, small round aluminum cake tins, paraffin or blocks of bees wax. The stick should be a little longer than the diameter of the tin and the string should be cut to a length a little longer than the height of the cake tin plus the allowance for tying it. Tie the string to the middle of the stick and palce horizontally over the rim of the tin. Allow to cool and set. Remove carefully from the tin and your candle is ready. Be very carefull, you'll need the help of an adult.

4.   Do you know of any temples that were rebuilt into churches?

....

....

5.   Make a mosaic. Using various colours of construction paper cut small squares of the same size. Draw a design on a piece of paper and glue the squares onto the design to fill it in. You can also use sanded down pieces of glass you've found on the beach. Glue these onto a clay design.

THE PERIOD
OF THE TURKISH OCCUPATION

1.   We find ourselves in the period of the Turkish Occupation. There's something in the illustration at the beginning of the chapter which shows this. Can you find it? ....

2.   In the illustration you'll also find some scattered fragments of an ancient temple. Circle them with your pencil.

3.   What do the letters stand for in the illustration on page 53?

4.   On a world map, find the cities abroad that Greeks settled in during the period of the Turkish Occupation.

5.   In the illustration below, the artist got a bit mixed up. There's something that doesn't belong to the period depicted. Can you find it? ....

THE EXCAVATION BEGINS...

1.   Look closely at the two illustrations at the beginning of the chapters, "From the cave era to the Neolitic revolution" and "The excavation begins". There are differences in the landscape. What caused them?

...AND THE SECRETS

1. Which periods are represented by each of the illustrations below? Look for clues in the large illustrations at the beginning of each chapter.

PERIODS:
Paleolithic period–Neolithic period–Mycenean period–Classical period–Roman period–Byzantine period–Turkish Occupation–Modern times.

ARE REVEALED

2.   Look closely at the illustration on pp 60-61. Which periods of time do you make out in the different layers? Start from the bottom up. You can do the same with the front cover of the book.

....

3.   Take some sand and form a hill. Set a temple on top of it, made out of sticks or sand and decorate it with stones, shells or branches.

4.   Next time you go to an archaeological museum, draw a picture of a jar or vessel like the girl is doing on page 57.

5.   In the stratigraphy of the excavation on page 60 see if you can make out the objects which characterize each period.

....

6.   Break a clay pot. After, try to glue the pieces back together like an archaeologist would.

A NEW BEGINNING AT THE NEOLITHIC SETTLEMENT

Exercise 1

1)   cutting wood
2)   ploughing
3)   breeding animals
4)   hunting
5)   fishing
6)   sifting flour
7)   baking bread
8)   pottery

CASTLES AND PALACES IN THE MYCENEAN ERA

Exercise 1

The false-spouted stirrup jar is D.

Exercise 2

scribe

BUILDING THE GREAT TEMPLE

Exercise 1

a)   carpenters, sculptors, transporters, engineers, architects, stone masons, crane operators, assisstants.
b)   boats and carts led by horses
c)   a crane
d)   the sculptor: hammer and chisel
       the engineers: compass and plumb bob
       the stone masons: sledge hammer and chisel

THE SPLENDID CITY OF THE CLASSICAL ERA

Exercise 1

Temple, portico, theatre, stadium, gymnasium, spring

THE GREAT DISASTER

Exercise 1

1)   a) Human factors: wars, invasions, pillaging
Natural disasters: earthquakes, volcanic eruptions, floods
3)   The Huns destroyed the Roman civilization
The Turks destroyed the Byzantine civilization

TO EXERCISES

The Western Europeans destroyed the people of pre-Columbian America

THE TEMPLE BECOMES A CHURCH
Exercise 1
1: Byzantine period or Early Christian period
2: 10 architectural fragments
4: The Parthenon → the Church of the Panagia
Temple of Hephaestus (or Theseion) → Church of St. George
Asclepeion on the south slope of the Acropolis → Church of Saints Anargyroi

THE PERIOD OF THE TURKISH OCCUPATION
Exercise 1
1. The mask and its minarets
2. Ἡ ἘλευθερίᾺ ῎Η ὁ ΘάνατοΣ (Freedom or Death)

THE EXCAVATION BEGINS
Exercise 1
The differences were caused by human intervention which was at times creative, but also destructive because of historical events.

...AND THE SECRETS ARE REVEALED
Exercise 1

Paleolithic period	prehistoric man
Neolithic period	fisherman, potter, oven
Mycenean period	scribe
Classical period	priest at the altar, the statue of Winged Victory, stadium
Roman period	soldier
Byzantine period	saint
Turkish Occupation	boat, mosque
Modern times	bus

Exercise 2
Cover page:

1) Paleolithic period	4) Byzantine period
2) Mycenean period	5) Turkish Occupation
3) Classical period	6) Modern times.

DOCUMENTATION - BIBLIOGRAPHY

This section of the book is mainly for use by older children, teachers and those interested in widening their knowledge of the subjects mentioned. Here we'll be documenting the information presented in the illustrations and texts. The facts are based on actual excavations or reasonable assumptions concluded from reliable ancient written sources. And of course there are some conjectures from the archaeologists' experienced approach to working with past events in the absence of documented facts. That way, even if the story here is, in part, imaginary, all the facts given could very well be true.

Archaeologists, who excavate in Greece and other parts of the world that have a long history, often come up against the phenomenon of successive habitations and destructions of one particular site. One of the mosta widely known cases is the ancient city of Troy because there is the problem of distinguishing which of the "seven successive cities" is the Homeric one. See in the catalogue of the exhibition, "Troy, Mycenae, Tiryns, Orhomeno. One hundred years after the death of Heinrich Schliemann" (1990).

Of course, choosing the periods mentioned in the book and what characterizes them is, in most part, assertive. Nowhere has there ever been found such a succession of findings in the exact same site. However, an uninterrupted succession of periods of time does exist in many areas of Greece, especially in the cases of Athens, Argos and Thebes where human activity never stoppd from the Neolithic period until today. Naturally, the type, the quantity and the quality of remains vary from time to time according to the significance of the specific area and the circumstances that followed. These factors dictated whether or not the older remains or ruins would be preserved or destroyed. For example, the prehistoric remains from the Acropolis in Athens are relatively few because of the extensive building activity on and around the "sacred rock" during the Archaic and Classical periods.

The choice of the architectural, as well as the cultural facts that are presented in the illustrations and text was made bearing in mind the specific characteristics of each period and their impact on historical development. For instance, in the Neolothic period the characteristics of agriculture and stock breeding economy is analyzed. Whereas, in the Mycenean acropolis what is analyzed is the economy of manufacturing and trade of the palace.

The idea for this book came from a small, but unique book by D. Tavernier, *Découverte d' une maison galloromaine* (1985) which S. Raftopoulou brought me from Paris. From the manner in which I fictionally narrated the first part of the book, I was greatly aided by reading the collective volume published by the Association of the study of Neo-Hellenic culture and general education under the title *One Day: Fifteen stories of daily life from ancient times to today"* (1988, in Greek). Also see corresponding works by D. Lipourlis, *He went to sleep at the Asclepeion of Epidaurus* (1992), as well as that of C.T. Panagos, *The diary of a 5th century B.C. businessman of Piraeus* (1994) (both in Greek).

The documention and bibliography can also be compared to the book by M. Korres, from *Pentelikon to the Parthenon* (1993) p. 62 or to the corresponding book by R. Scranton-J. Shaw-L. Ibrahim, *Kenchreai; Eastern port of Korinth I* (1978) appendix F. which has a drawing of the port and to the colour plates of A. McBride in the book of N. Sekunda *The Army of Alexander the Great* (1984). But because any other documentation would require a specalized bibliography, making the book difficult to use for the general public, I restricted myself to general references and accessible books and articles. In some instances, however, I could not resist adding some specialized bibliography.

For the prehistoric, Byzantine and modern period I was supported by my friends and colleagues C. Boulotis S. Kalopissi, N. Gioles and M. Euthymious who filled in some gaps in the bibliography. C.

Boulotis also kindly read all the text and commented on the content and style of writing. E. Baziotopoulou did much work on the rough draft and gave the book its title. Finally, I must thank and congratulate A. Ganosi for giving such life to the book with her exquisite illustrations which make reading the book more pleasurable.

FROM THE CAVE ERA TO THE NEOLITHIC REVOLUTION

Here, one of the most significant developments in the history of mankind, conventionally called the Neolithic Revolution, is presented figuratively and simplified. It was a long process which led primitive man to change the basic way he obtained his food. From a wandering food gatherer and hunter, he became a permanent resident of an area and produced his own food by cultivating wheat and domesticating animals. For detailed information on the presuppositions and consequences of this development, and also the archaeological data from the Middle East where it is thought that this first took place, see the book by V. Gordon Childe, *Man Makes Himself* (1956).

Although a reputable source, the book is somewhat outdated when compared to more recent research. Also see the book by G. Clark-S. Piggot, *Pre-historic Societies*.

The chapter opens with a narration of the lifestyle of the pre-Neolitic era and the events we believe led to the Neolithic Revolution. There is a descrepancy in the research as to whether the cultivation of land and the domestication of animals followed permanent settlement or if it presupposed it. I don't think we can ever be sure of such things. These developments were very slow and more than likely took place simultaneously in differen parts of the Middle East. This therefore does not allow for generalization and lends only theoretical value to the views of archaeologists.

In general we must bear in mind that historical, social and all other changes that took place in ancient times were very slow and cannot be compared to today's pace of how things change. The more we go back in time, the slower the developments took place. Thus, one year in our time could be equivalent to a century in the classical era and more than a thousand or thousands of years in pre-historic times. As a result, the Neolithic Revolution must have lasted many centuries in one place, while it might have taken thousands of years for the Neolithic Revolution to spread to other places. The time span in our story in this book has been shortened to two or three generations.

For a quick examination of the archaeological facts for the pre-Neolithic stage of Greek pre-history see the books by D. Theoharis, *Neolithic Greece* (1973) page 17ff., and *Neolithic Civilization* (1981) page 15 ff. For details about the paleolithic settlement in the cave of Kleidi in the Aoos Valley in Epirus as well as other paleolithic settlements in Greece, see G. Kourtessi-Philippaki, *Le paléolithique de la Grèce continentale* (1986) and the four volumes of the periodical Ἀρχαιολογία, 1996 (in Greek). For the first tribes of Greek pre-history and their origin see M. Sakellariou, *Peuples prehélléniques et origine Indoeuropéene* (1977). C. Renfrew in his book *Archaeology and Language. The puzzle of Indoeuropean Origins* (1987), rejects the existence of an Indo-european race which is generally believed to have arrived in Greece in the third millennium B.C. He claims that the inhabitants of neolithic Greece were in fact "Greeks" who had settled here from the Middle East, from where they brought farming and stock-breeding. For a critique of this theory see M.B. Sakellariou's *The Origin of the Indoeuropeans. A critique of new theories*, N.P. Goulandris Foundation. *Museum of Cycladic* Art. Lectures 1986-1989 (1990) page 135 ff. (in Greek).

A NEW BEGINNING AT THE NEOLITHIC SETTLEMENT

This chapter depicts the structure and activities of a typical Neolithic village (6000-3000 B.C.). The model for the illustration was taken from the representative drawings of the settlement of Dimini and Sesklos in Thessaly and were created by M. Korres for the books of D. Theoharis (cited before). These books contain the best collection of evidence of the Neolithic period, especially in Thessaly. For the most current facts from all of Greece, see the catalogue of exhibitions from the Goulandris Museum, G. Papathanasopoulos (ed.), Neolithic Culture (1996). Specifically for Neolithic Attica see the books by M. Pantelidou which refer to the excavations in Nea Makri, no. 1, *Constructions* (1991) and no 2, *Pottery* (1995), both in Greek.

For details about obsidian and evidence of earlier existence in Aegean trade, see Ἀρχαιολογία *32,* 1989 p. 11 ff. For the religious perceptions of the people at that time, as much as can be researched, mainly from figurines, see G. Hourmouziades, *The Human-shaped Figurines of Neolithic Thessaly* (1973), (in Greek), K. Gallis-L. Orphanidis, *Figurines of Neolithic Thessaly* (1996), D. Theoharis, *Neolithic Greece* (1973), and Ἀρχαιολογία vol. 34 (1990) p. 17 ff. and vol. 38 (1991) p. 44 ff. For earthquakes which we know that occurred in Greec in the past, see V. and K. Papazachou, *The Earthquakes of Greece* (1989) (in Greek) and S. Stiros-R.E. Jones (eds.) *Archaeoseismology* (1996).

CASTLES AND PALACES IN THE MYCENEAN ERA

The third chapter presents Mycenean Greece of the so-called Late Bronze Age and more specifically the Late Helladic III period (1400-1100 B.C.) which was a time where Mycenean civilization was most widespread, characterized by two architectural elements – Cyclopean citadels and palaces.

The illustration of the walls and the palace is a partial representation of the acropolis of Mycenae. The most simplified presentation of the elements of Mycenean civilization and especially its capital, Mycenae, is found in the book by G. Mylonas, *Mycenae: Rich in Gold* (1983), as well as in the catalogue of the exhibition *The Mycenean world. Five centuries of early Hellenic civilization (1600-1100 B.C.)* (1988). For a more detailed approach to the archaeological facts concerning the Bronze Age, see F. Vermeule, *Greece in the Bronze Age* (1972)[2], O. Dickinson, *The Aegean Bronze Age* (1994), and lastly, R. Trenil and others, *Les Civilization Égeenenes* (1989) with a full bibliography. For Cyprus in the Bronze Age and the production of bronze see V. Karagiorges, *The Civilization of Pre-historic Cyprus* (1975). For the manufacturing and trade of scented oil see C.V. Shelmerdine, *The Perfume Industry of Mycenean Pylos* (1985). For the weaving of cloth by the Cretans, we simply refer to a Linear B tablet from Knossos on which is recorded that 100.000 castrated male sheep were fed for the sole purpose of wool production.

For Minoan Crete and its conquest by the Myceneans around 1450 B.C., see the bibliography in R. Trenil and others, *Les Civilization Égeennes.* For the excavation of the two shipwrecks of the Mycenean period on the shores of Asia Minor in Gelidonya and Ulu-Burun, see G.F. Bass, *Cape Gelidonya. A Bronze Age Shipwreck* (1967) and *A Bronze Age Shipwreck at Ulu-Burun* (Kas) (1984) by the same author. For shipwrecks in general, see P. Throckmorton, *Shipwrecks and Archaeology* (1970) and Ἀρχαιολογία vol. 8 (1983). Important information about sea voyages in ancient times was obtained from the construction of "Cyreneia II" a replica of the original ship from the 4th century B.C. which was pulled out of the sea of Cyreneia, Cyprus. The "Cyreneia II" simulated the ancient voyage of the original ship. See more in the catalogue of the exhibition, *Travelling with the ship of Cyreneia in tme and myth,* (1987). In general for ships and sea voyages in the ancient world, see O. Höckmann, *Antike Seefahrt* (1985). For the ancient ships of all the Mediterranean peoples see L. Basch, *Le Musée imaginaire de la marine antique* (1987) and S.S. Morrison, *Greek and Roman Oared Warships, 399-30 B.C.* (1996).

For the Linear B tablets and their decipherment by M. Ventris and J. Chadwick, see the latter's book, *The Decipherment of Linear B* (1967) and J.T. Hooker, *An Introduction to Linear B* (1980). In general for all early writings, see the catalogue of the exhibition *The birth of writing* (1990) which was published by the Centre for Educational Programmes of the Greek Ministry of Culture.

For the historicity of the Trojan War and, in general, the Homeric poems, see Joachim Latacz, *Homer, His Art and His World* [1](1996) trans. by J.P. Holska, Hilary Mackie *Talking Trojan* (1996) and the proceedings of the conference of L. Foxhall-J. Davies (eds.), *The Trojan War. Its historicity and context* (1981). For the destruction of the Mycenean palaces and the fall of the Mycenean civilization, see R. Drews, *The End of the Bronze Age* (1933). For the relationship between the Mycenean king and the leaders of Asia Minor at that time, as is indicated from letters found in the archives of the Hittites, see M. Mellink, *The Hittites and the Aegean World*, American Journal of Archaeology 87, 1983, p. 133 ff. For the so-called People of the Sea, see T. and M. Dothan, *People of the Sea*, (1992). The illustration of the sea vessel was an inspiration from the miniature wall painting of ships found at Akrotiri, Thera and is exhibited in the National Archaeological Museum of Athens. For details, see S. Marinatos, *The Excavation of Thera IV* (1974) and Ch. Doumas, T*he Wall Paintings of Thera* (1992).

THE BUILDING OF THE GREAT TEMPLE

The description of how a temple was built in the Classical period of Greece (500-300 B.C.) is an effort to present the structure and function of Athenian democracy. On this subject there is sufficient evidence from written sources (both ancient writers and inscriptions) and from archaeological conclusions, especially those from the excavations of the Athenian Acropolis and the ancient Agora. See C.L. Mossé, *Histoire d' une Democratie. Athénes* (1971) and J. DeRomilly, *Problem de la democratie grecque* (1975). For the birth of Athenian democracy, see Ch. Starr, *The Birth of Greek Democracy* (1990) J. Thorley, *Athenian Democracy* (1996), J. Ober-Ch. Hedrick, *Demokratia: A Conversation on Democracies, Ancient and Modern* (1996), Thomas Martin, *Ancient Greece* (1996), H.D. Amos and A.G.P. Lang, *Those were the Greeks* (1996), Michael Grant, *The Classical Greeks* (1996) and the catalogue of the exhibition which took place at the American School of Classical Studies (1993) on the occasion of the 2500-year anniversary of that event.

The illustration is clearly influenced by the illustrations 19-22 from the book *From Pantelikon to the Parthenon* by M. Korres (1993). The temple described is none other than the so-called pre-

Parthenon, that is, the temple that started being built after the Battle of Marathon (490 B.C.) as a tribute to the victory of the battle. The construction was interrupted 5 to 6 years later. It had reached a height up to the second or third drum of the columns and its remains were destroyed by the fire set by Xerxes when he invaded Athens a little before the famous sea battle of Salamis (480 B.C.), Herodotus 8, 51-53. To see the final design the temple would have had before its destruction by the Persians, see the previously mentioned book by M. Korres, illustration 21.

Most of the information and evidence in the text is taken from what is already known about the Parthenon of Pericles and the other Classical buildings of the Acropolis. *Related facts* about the reconstruction of the Parthenon of Pericles are described in the book by Plutarch, *The Life of Pericles,* paragraph 12 ff. In paragraph 14, there is reference to the reaction of the political opposition of Thucydides of Melisios who claimed that decorating Athens with such magnificent monuments would be like hanging jewellery on an arrogant woman. From the same text we are informed about an accident that happened during the construction of the Propylaea.

Of course it is implied that the architect who undertook the building project was Phidias who, himself, was not an architect. But we are sure that his advice in the concept and final design of the temple was a determining factor. Phidias also supervised the construction; he was the "overseer of all on behalf of his frienship with Pericles". It is unfortunate that in our modern world we do not have the same criteria that the ancient world did in choosing a constructor for public works. Plutarch in his *Ethics* 3, 498 E names the criteria: the quality of construction, the cost of the project and the time it takes for completion.

Tiryns and Mycenae are two other sites, besides Athens, where a temple has been built on Mycenean ruins. The uninterrupted continuation between the Mycenean and Hellenic periods is characterized by the fact that the historical core of most of the Greek myths is found in the Mycenean period and refers to the dynasty of kings in these areas. For the transference of the older elements of Greek culture to the next generations, see A Toynbee, *The Greeks and their Heritage* (1981).

In general, for ancient Greek temples and their characteristics see I. Phoka-P. Valavanis, *Architecture and City Planning* (1992) page 78 ff.; specifically for the Parthenon, see page 86 ff. For a complete presentation of the history and art of this monument see the collected work: *The Parthenon and its Impact in Modern Times* (1994). To find out more about how public buildings were constructed see specifically J.J Coulton, *Greek Architects at Work* (1977). For the building material, tools and processing of materials see A. Orlandos, *The building material of the ancient Grakks I+II* (in Greek) and for the Roman times, J.P. Adam, *La Construction Romaine* (1989).

For details about sacrifices for foundations of ancient buildings see F. van Straten, *Images of Animal Sacrifice in Archaic and Classical Greece.* (1994). The ancient Greeks believed it was not a good omen when the sacrificial animals resisted so strongly. For strikes in ancient times see X. Thomaides *The Strike in the Ancient Greek period* (in Greek) in the Proceedings of the XVIII International Congress of Papyrology (1986).

Water projects (dams, canals ets) were found in Greece, especially in the area of Copais, Boiotia in the second millennium B.C. see J. Knauss, *Die Melioration desKopaisbeckens durch die Minyer im 2. Jt v. Chr.* (1987). For equivalent projects of Greek engineers in the Egyptian interior, see E.G. Turner, *Greek Papyri. An Introduction* (1968) page 71 ff. For ancient Greek technology and its progress, see Ch. Singer, E. Holmyard, A.R. Hall (eds), A History of Technology I. *From Early Times to the Fall of Ancient Empires* (1995) and J. G. Landels, *Engineering in the Ancient Word* (1978).

An equivalent example of the destruction of walls for the purpose of constructing public works can be seen in the decision of the emperor of the eastern Roman empite, Valens (364/65 A.D.), to use the material of the walls of Chalcedon to construct the great aquaduct of Constantinople.

THE SPLENDID CITY OF THE CLASSICAL ERA

The illustration here represents a typical image of an ancient Greek city from the Classical era to Roman times (500 B.C. - 330 A.D.), as well as the daily activities of its residents. Almost all of the cities of the Classical, Hellenistic and Roman times were constructed, most of the time, without any proper organized city planning. Exceptions to the rule were the cities designed and constructed under the Hippodamean System (for example Miletos, Piraeus, Rhodes), where the system for a rectangular road network made the city well-defined. For city planning in ancient Greece, see IEE vol. ΓΖ, page 328 ff. and vol. E. page 469 ff. Also see I. Phoka-P. Valavanis, *Architecture and City Planning* (1996)². General reference books on the subject are: R. Martin, L' *Urbanism dans la Grèce antique* (1956), R. E. Wycherley, *How the Greeks Built Cities*, (1976) and W. Hoepfner-E.L. Schwandner, *Haus und Stadt im antiken Griecheland* (1986). Also, R. Tomlison, *From Mycenae to Constantinople. The Evolution of the Greek City* (1992).

An example of a temple built on a hill with an agora (market place) at its foothills is in Athens with the temple of Hephaestus (Theseion) at the top of Agoraios Kolonos, west of the Classical Agora of the city. For the construction of the Agora of Athens, the best known agora of the ancient world, see J.M. Camp, *The Athenian Agora. Ecavations in the Heart of Classical Athens* (1986) H. Thompson-

J.M. Camp, *The Athenian Agora, A Guide* (1990)[4]. For the political organization of ancient Greek cities, see G. Glotz, *La Cité grecque* (1953)[2]. For daily activities of private and public life, see T.B.L. Webster, *Athenian Culture and Society* (1973).

For ancient religion, celebrations and worship, see (IEE) B page 66 ff. and vol. ΓΖ, page 248 ff., M. Nilsson, *A History of Greek Religion* (1967), R. Martin-H. Metzger, *La Réligion gréque* (1976) and N. Burkert, *Greek Religion* (1985). For mythology, see I. Kakrides (ed.), *Greek Mythology* (1986). And lastly, W. Burkert, *Structure and History in Greek Mythology and Ritual* (1979). For tourists who were educated in antiquity and who recorded their impressions, see Αρχαιολογία vol. 3 (1992) p. 22 ff. and L. Casson, *Travel in the Ancient World* (1974). Among the most admired objects were the cult-statues of the ancient temples, especially those of gold and ivory like the goddess Athena in the Parthenon and Zeus in the temple of Olympia, both carved by Phidias in the third quarter of the 5th c. B.C.

For the wooden tables in the Eastern building of the Athenian Agora, see H. Thompson, *Hesperia* 22, 1953 p. 36 ff. For general information on banks and the bank system in antiquity, see R. Bogaert, *Banques et banquiers dans Les cités grécques* (1968). For inflation, see X. Thomaides, *Inflation in Antiquity* (1993) (in greek). For the inscriptions and their importance for the ancient people see B.F. Cook, *Greek Inscriptions* (1987) and Ἀρχαιολογία vol 5, 1982 p. 65 ff. and vol. 6, 1983 p. 50 ff.

The best red mullets in antiquity were fished in the sea of the Aixonides (today, Glyfada). They were famous and were referred to by the ancient connoisseurs as the "Aixonidian mullets". The best source for the diet of the ancient Greeks is the book by Atheneus, *Dipnosophistae*. For general information, also see Ἀρχαιολογία vol. 2, 1989, p. 91 and vol. 28, 1988 p. 71 ff. and A. Dalby, *Siren Feasts. A History of Food and Gastronomy in Ancient Greece* (1996).

For the daily activities and any kind of event that took place in the ancient Athenian Agora, see the small illustrated books of the American School of Classical Studies, *Picture Books*. For general information on the economic and social conditions in ancient Greece, see M. I. Finley, *Economy and Society in Ancient Greece I, II* (Greek trans. 1988, 1991); and for slavery, see Y. Garlan, *Slavery in Ancient Greece* (1988).

The transport of entire buildings was not unusual, as was not the phenomenon of pre-fabricated buildings. See M. Korres, *Bauplannung und Bautheorie der Antike* (1983) p. 201 ff.

For the life of children see M. Golden, *Children and Childhood in Classical Athens* (1990). For children's games see R. Schmidt, *Die Darstellung von Kinderspielzeug und Kinderspiel in der gr. Kunst*, and the catalogue of the exhibition of Marseilles, *Jouer dans l' Antiquité* (1991). For the position of women see A. Cameron-A. Kuhrt (eds), *Images of Women in Antiquity* (1983) and E. Fantham (ed), *Women in the Classical World* (1994). For how the ancient Greeks dressed, see E. Abrahams-L. Evans, *Ancient Greek Dress* (1964) and G. Losfeld, *Essai sur le Costume Grecq* (1991).

For the education of the young, and physical training, see F. Beck, *Album of Greek Education* (1975) and H.I. Marrou, *History of Education in Antiquity* (1956). For general information on this topic see Ἀρχαιολογία vol. 25, 1987. Specifically for the training and education of adolescents, see Ἀρχαιολογία vol. 35, 1990 p. 64. Theoretical education germinated in the ancient gymnasiums and continued to grow until the 5th century A.D. where they ceased to operate. It is not by chance, therefore, that many names of educational cultural institutions in the modern world come from the ancient gymnasiums of Athens such the Lyceum and the Academia.

For ancient theatre see M. Bieber, *The History of the Greek and the Roman Theatre* (1961)[2], A. Pickard-Cambridge, *The Dramatic Festival of Athens* (1988)[3], E. Simon, *The Ancient Theatre* (1982) and R. Green-E. Hanley, *Images of the Greek Theatre* (1995). For athletics see H.A. Harris, *Sport in Greece and Rome* (1972) as well as the catalogue of the exhibition, "Mind and Body", (Athens 1989).

THE GREAT DISASTER

The illustration depicts the destruction of a city, the result of barbaric invasions in the provinces of the Roman empire, especially in the 3rd century A.D. In this particular case, the city could very well have been Athens, which in 267 A.D., was attacked and set on fire by the Herulians and Goths.

The story gives us a chance to see what the Greco-Roman world was like during the first few centuries A.D. and what the relationship was between the Greeks and Romans. For a description of Greece during that time see P. Grimal et alii, *Hellenism and the Rise of Rome* (1968).

The looting of Greek treasures started quite early, when the Romans first invaded Greek territory. The forerunner was Flamininus who defeated the Macedonian king, Phillip V at Cynoscephalae in 197 B.C. Polybius, the historian, criticizes this (9, 3, 10). Many works of art and sacred objects from ancient Greek cities and sanctuaries were also taken by Sulla in 86 B.C. Looting became a common practice for emperors, specifically Nero who travelled throughout Greece in 66 B.C. For general information see M. Pape, *Griechische Kunstwerke und ihre öffentliche Ausstellung in rom* (1975). Many of the ships laden with works of art sank because of the heavy load, thus most of the Greek bronze statues have been found in the depths of the seas. e.g. Zeus or Poseidon of Artemisium, an adolescent from Antikythera, a young boy of Marathon, the Riace statues.

Changes in the structure of theatres in the post-Roman times are related to changes in their use (e.g. arenas, pools, etc.). This also occurred in the orchestra of the theatre of Dionysos in Athens. For details, see J. Travlos, *The Pictorial Dictionary of Ancient Athens*, (1980) p. 537 and on. For the re-utilization of old statues in Roman times see H. Blanck, *Wiederverwendung alter Statuen als Ehrendenkmähler bei Grechen und Römer* (1969).

The defense of ancient cities at that time was quite insufficient. An example of this is the fact that in Athens, Dexippus could only muster up 2000 men in the defense against the Herulians. The construction of defense walls with ready material was very common during difficult and urgent times in the history of Greece. Characteristic of this is the reconstruction of the Themistoclean surrounding wall of Athens in 479 B.C. right after the departure of the Persians, (see Thucydides 1, 90, 3 and 1, 93, 3; Plutarch, Themistocles 19, 1). The wall referred to in the text is the so-called Valerianeum, built under the auspices of the emperor Valerian (253-256 A.D.) to protect the city against invasions.

Many temples in the area of the sanctuary of Olympius were demolished in order to build this wall. See Travlos, (op.cit) pp. 335, 429. The same thing happened a few years later with the construction of the so-called post-Roman wall which the Athenians who survived built from the ruins of public buildings destroyed by the Herulians, see Thompson-Camp, op.cit, p. 142 ff.

For the setting on fire of the Acropolis, supposedly by the Herulians see I. Travlos, Ἀρχαιολογικὴ Ἐφημερίς 1973, p. 218 ff. (in Greek). For the probable condition of the interior of the Parthenon after the fire damage, see the drawings which accompany the article by M. Korres, "The Parthenon from antiquity until the 19th century" in the book. *The Parthenon and its Impact in Modern Times* (1994), p. 141. For burial customs and their development throughout the ancient world, see J. Boardman-D. Kurtz, *Greek Burial Customs* (1991) and R. Garland, *The Greek Way of Death* (1985).

THE TEMPLE BECOMES A CHURCH

There are two periods of the Byzantine era presented in this chapter: 1. the paleo-Christian centuries (4th to 6th c. A.D.) and 2. the Early and mid-Byzantine centuries (7th to 12th c. A.D.). The first period, a time of great changes, was a midpoint between the ancient world and the Christian world. See P. Brown, *The World of Late Antiquity. From Aurelius to Muhammed* (1976), G. Bowerstock, *Hellenism in Late Antiquity* (1990) and M. Sordi, *The Christians and the Roman Empire* (1994).

Athens served as a bulwark of ethnic spirit because of its classical tradition and its schools of philosophy. See T.L. Shear, *Athens. From City-State to Provincial Town*, Hesperia, 50, 1981, pp. 356-377/ P. Castrin, *Post-Herulian Athens* (1994). The idol worshippers and the Christians lived in harmony in Athens at that time. This is exemplified by the fact that Erculius, governor of the province of Illyricum, apportioned the great library of Hadrian, the largest cultural foundation of Athens, to both the idol worshippers and the Christians for common use. See Travlos, op. cit. p. 244 ff.

For the ancient Greek temples which became Christian churches see A. Franz, *From Paganism to Christianity in the Temples of Athens*, Dumbarton Oaks Papers 19 (1965) pp. 187-205. For the transformation of the Parthenon to a Christian temple and the changes to its structure, see M. Korres-Ch. Bouras, *Studies of the Restoration of the Parthenon* (1983) p. 138 ff. (in Greek), M. Korres, "The Parthenon from ancient times until the 19th century", in the book *The Parthenon and its Impact in Modern Times* (1994) p. 136 ff.

The Parthenon was initially changed into the Temple of the Wisdom of God, and later to the temple of the Panagia. Another example is the church which was built upon the ruins of the Asclepieion, the sacred sanatorium located on the southern slope of the Acropolis. Its name was changed to honour the memory of the Christian doctors, saints Anargyroi. For the orders of the Byzantine emperor on the ancient Greek temples see A. Franz, *Late Antiquity: A.D. 267-700. The Athenian Agora XXIV* (1988). p. 69 ff. For details on the destruction of ancient temples by fanatic Christians, especially in Asia Minor, Syria and Egypt, see F.W. Deichmann, *Erühchristliche Kirchen in antiken Heiligthümer*, Jd. I 54, 1939, p. 105 ff. (where 89 transformations to Christian churches are mentioned) and J. Vaes, "Christliche Wiederewendung antiker Bauten". *Ancient Society* 15-17 (1984-86) pp. 305-443.

For the paleo-Christian basilica churches and their architectural characteristics, see G. J. Davies, *The Origin and Development of Early Christian Architecture* (1952) and R. Krantheimer, *Early Christian and Byzantine Architecture* (1986)³. These older churches did not have an iconostas but rather, short marble screen panels. Higher wooden iconostasis appeared in the 14th century.

For the history of Byzantium during the mid-Byzantine period, see G. Ostrogorsky, *History of the Byzantine State* (1956). For mid-Byzantine art see L. Rodley, *Byzantine Art and Architecture. An Introduction* (1994). For the plan of wall paintings of the churches at that time see V. Lazarev, *Storia della Pitture bizantina* (1967) and C. Delvoye, *Byzantine Art.* (1976).

THE PERIOD OF THE TURKISH OCCUPATION

This chapter briefly describes the course of Hellenism during the Turkish occupation with specific emphasis on some unfamiliar points related to the ancient world. For the subjects elaborated on see, sir Steven Runciman, *The Great Church in Captivity* (1968), P. Sugar, *Southeastern Europe under Ottoman Rule, 1354-1804* (1977), and R. Clogg, *A Concise History of Greece* (1992).

The reconstruction of country churches on the sites of ruined churches during the Turkish occupation is a common phenomenon. The Christians re-utilized ancient statues by engraving a cross on them. For details see A. Delivorrias, *Interpretatio Christiana, to Eyphrosynon*, a work dedicated to Hatzidakis (1991) p. 107 ff. For details about using the engraved Classical tombstone of Phrasicleïa as an icon in an Athenian church during the Turkish occupation, see G. Despinis, periodical *Egnatia* vol. 3, 1991-1992 p. 57 and especially p. 62 ff. (in Greek).

THE EXCAVATION BEGINS... AND THE SECRETS ARE REVEALED

The illustration of the hill next to the beach and, in general, the excavation site I refer to in the text, is based on an actual mound. This mound is called Xeropolis, in Lefkandi, Euboia, a village berween Halkis and Eretria next to Vasiliko. Here a high hill was formed from the successive inhabitation and destruction of a series of settlements from the early Helladic period (2100 B.C.) up to and including the Geometric era (8th cent. B.C.). English and Greek archaeologists excavated this mound by digging in at a depth of 17 metres, the deepest cut made into Greek territory up until now. For details, see M.R. Popham-L.H. Sackett, *Lefkandi I, The Iron Age. The Settlement* (1980).

Blegen, who is mentioned in the text, is the American archaeologist, Carl Blegen, who in 1939 just before world War II, discovered 600 clay tablets in the archives of the Mycenean palace of Nestor at Pylos. See C. Blegen-M. Rausson-W.D. Taylour-W. Donovan, *The Palace of Nestor at Pylos in Western Messenia I-III* (1966-1973).

From the rich foreign bibliography on the techniques of excavation, I will only mention Ph. Barker, *The Techniques of Archaeological Excavation* (1977) and D.G. Dever, *A Manual of Field Excavation* (1978). For the history of restoration of ancient Greek monuments, see V. Petrakos (ed.), *Greek Restorations* (1996) (in Greek). Specifically for the works in the Acropolis, see R. Economakis (ed), *Acropolis Restoration: The CCAM Inervention* (1994).

The archaeologists have named the soil where there is no trace of human elements, as "virgin". This soil usually consists of natural rock of sand deposits which are a result of geological factors.

The archaeological periodicals which contain the publication of preliminary exhibitions of excavations are: Ἀρχαιολογικόν Δελτίον [Archaeological Bulletin] of the Greek Archaeological Service, Ἔργον [Ergon] and its Πρακτικά [Proceedings] from the Archaeological Society of Athens. Parallel information can be found in the periodicals issued by the Fench and British School of Archaeology in Athens; that is, in Chronique des fovilles of Bulletin de Correspondance Hellenique and in Archaeological Reports of the British School Annual.

For the history and the study of classical archaeology in Greece, see M. Schanks, *Classical Archaeology of Greece. Experiences of the Discipline* (1996). General information and critiques on the current situation in Greece as far as archaeology is concerned can be found in A. Zoes, *Archaeology in Greece. Its Problems and Perspectives* (1990) (in Greek).

CHRONOLOGICAL TABLE
OF THE HISTORY OF GREECE

Paleolithic era ....600.000(?) – 8000B.C.

Mesolithic–neolithic era ....8000 – 3000 B.C.

Bronze age ....3000 – 1100 B.C.

Mycenean period ....1600 – 1100 B.C.

Protogeometric and
Geometric period ....1100 – 700 B.C.

Archaic period ....700 – 500 B.C.

Classical period..500 – 300 B.C.

Hellenistic period ....300 – 1st cent. B.C.

Roman period ....1st cent. B.C. – 330 A.D.

Byzantine period...330 – 1453 A.D.

Turkish occupation ....1453 – 1821 A.D.

Modern Greece ....1821 – today

Panos Valavanis, *The Hill of the Hidden Secrets*

Illustrated by Ada Ganosi

Activities by Mariza Decastro, Panos Valavanis

Typesetting and front cover: LineArt, Efessou 24,
171 21 N. Smyrni, tel.: 210-9310 766, fax: 210-9314 918

Translated and Proofread by Georgia Kofinas, tel.: 210-9316 087

Production supervision: Makrigiannis & Sons CO.
Notara 117 & Skouze, 185 35 Piraeus, tel.: 210-4280 070, fax: 210-4280 071

© Panos Valavanis, Akritas Publications

First English edition: April 1998
Fourth edition: April 2004

Δ 4 04 ΑΠ 56 266

ISBN: 960-328-103-4

ΕΚΔΟΣΕΙΣ ΑΚΡΙΤΑΣ AKRITAS PUBLICATIONS
24 Efessou str., 171 21 N. Smyrni,
tel.: 210-9334 554, 9314 968, fax: 210-9311 436
5 Pesmatzoglou str., 104 65 Athens, tel.: 210-3247 678
5 Tsimiski str., 546 25 Thessaloniki, tel. and fax: 2310-540610
E-mail: info@akritas.net.gr   www.akritas.net.gr